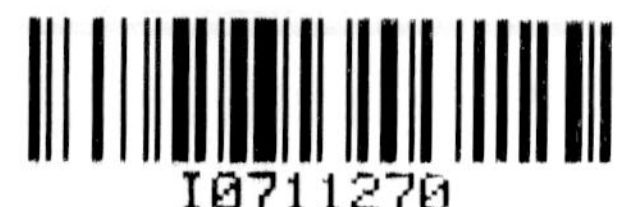

this book belongs to :

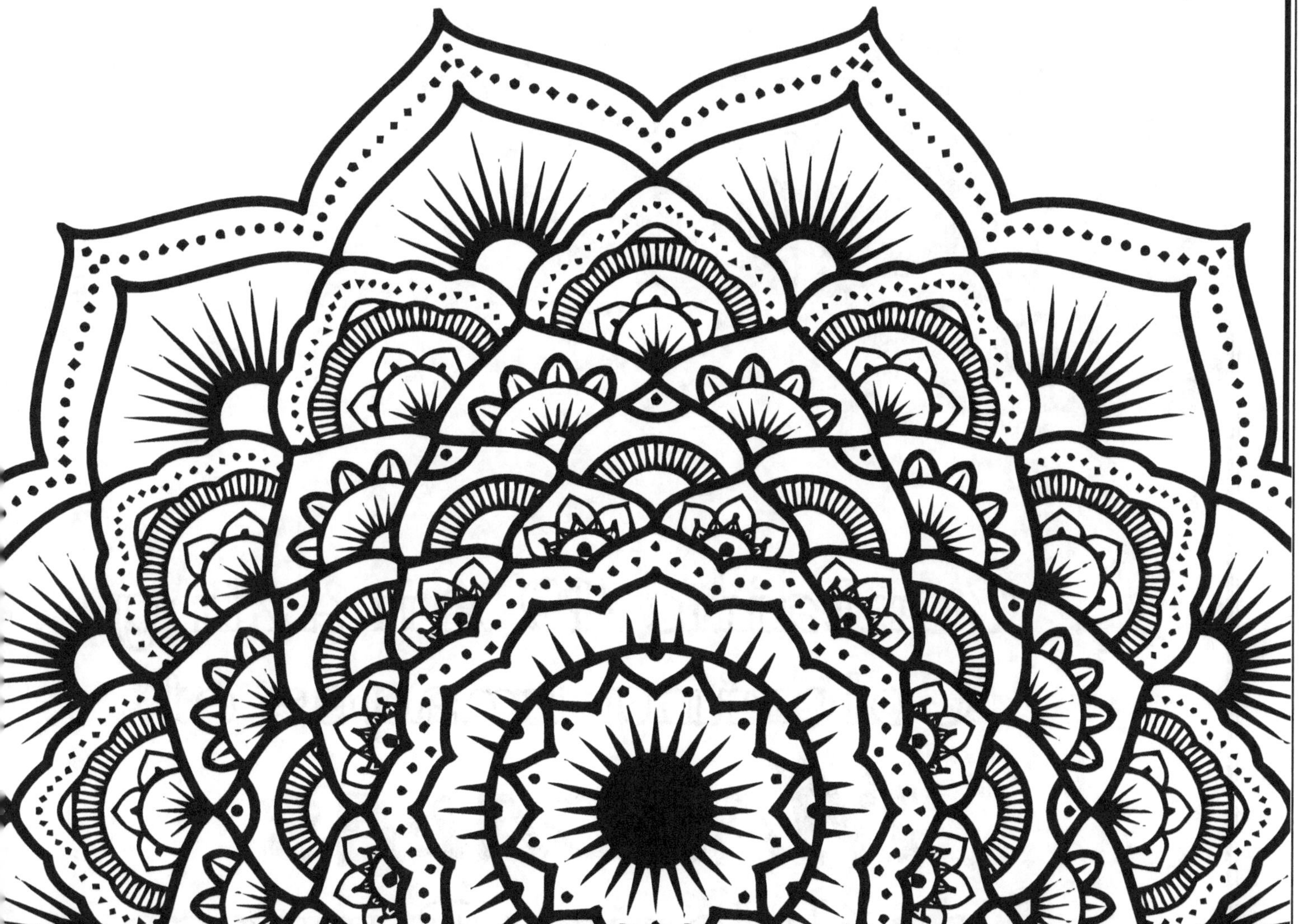

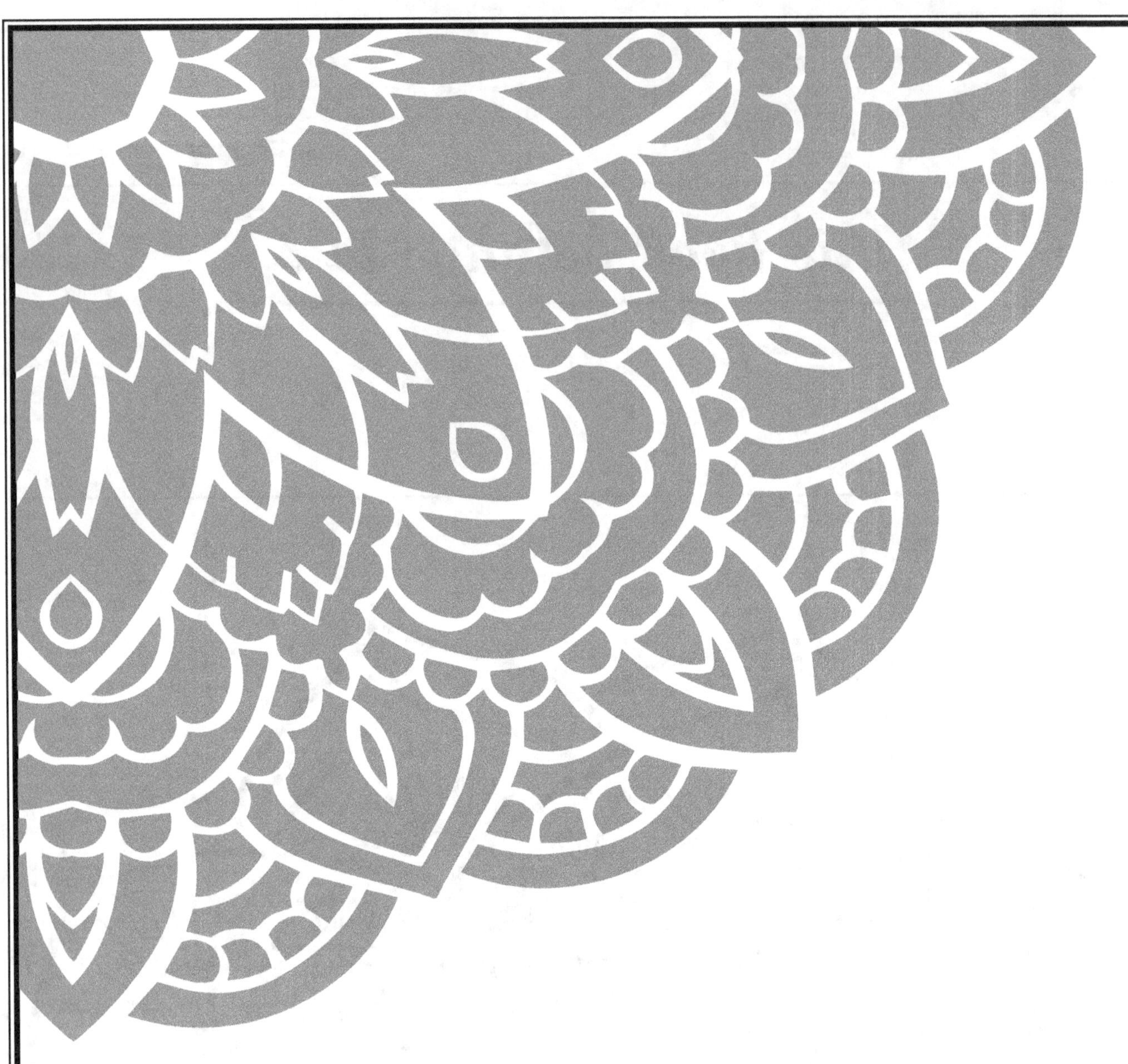

Contains 49 Amazing
Coloring Images of
MANDALAS
For Coloring Purpose

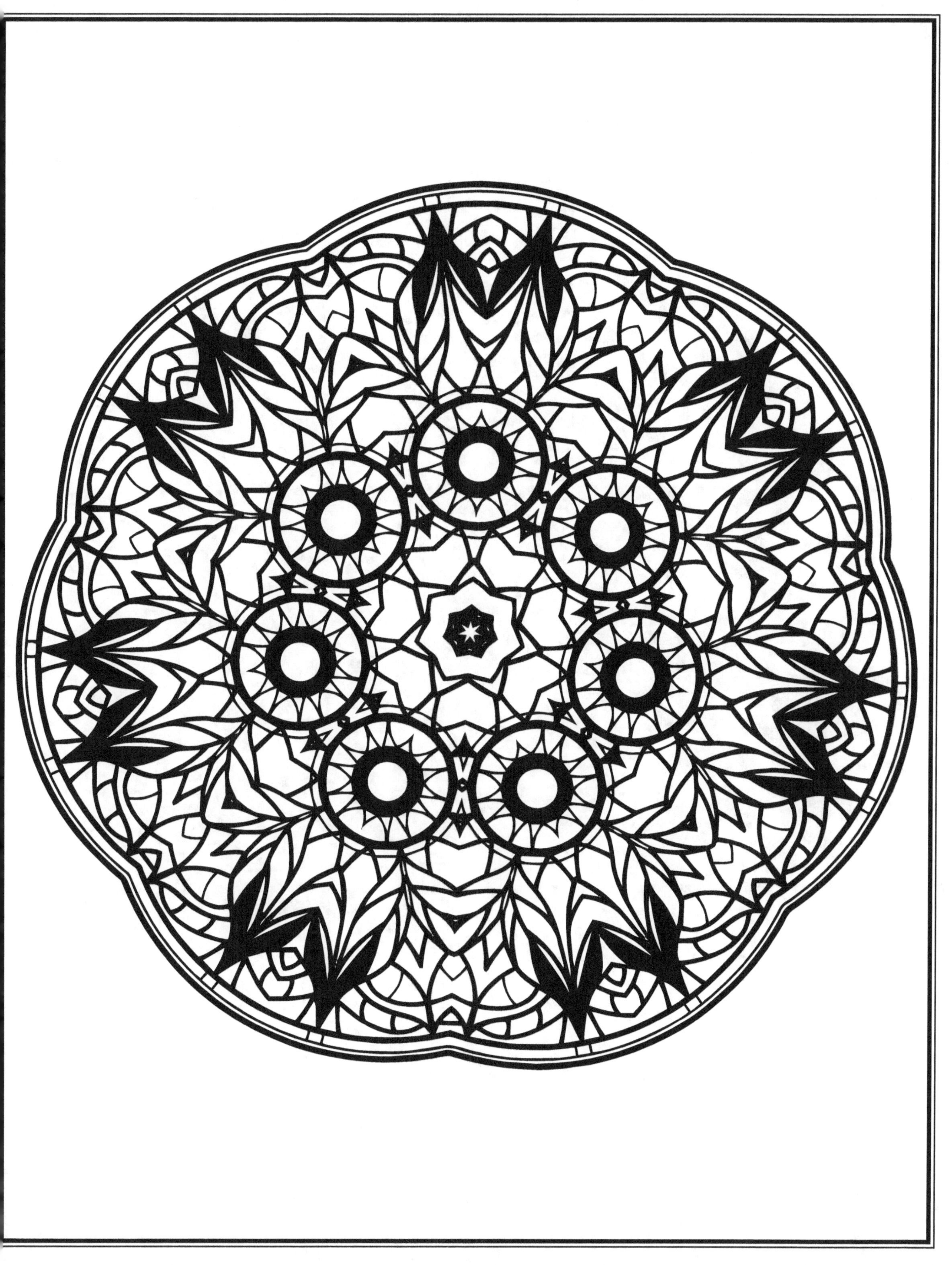

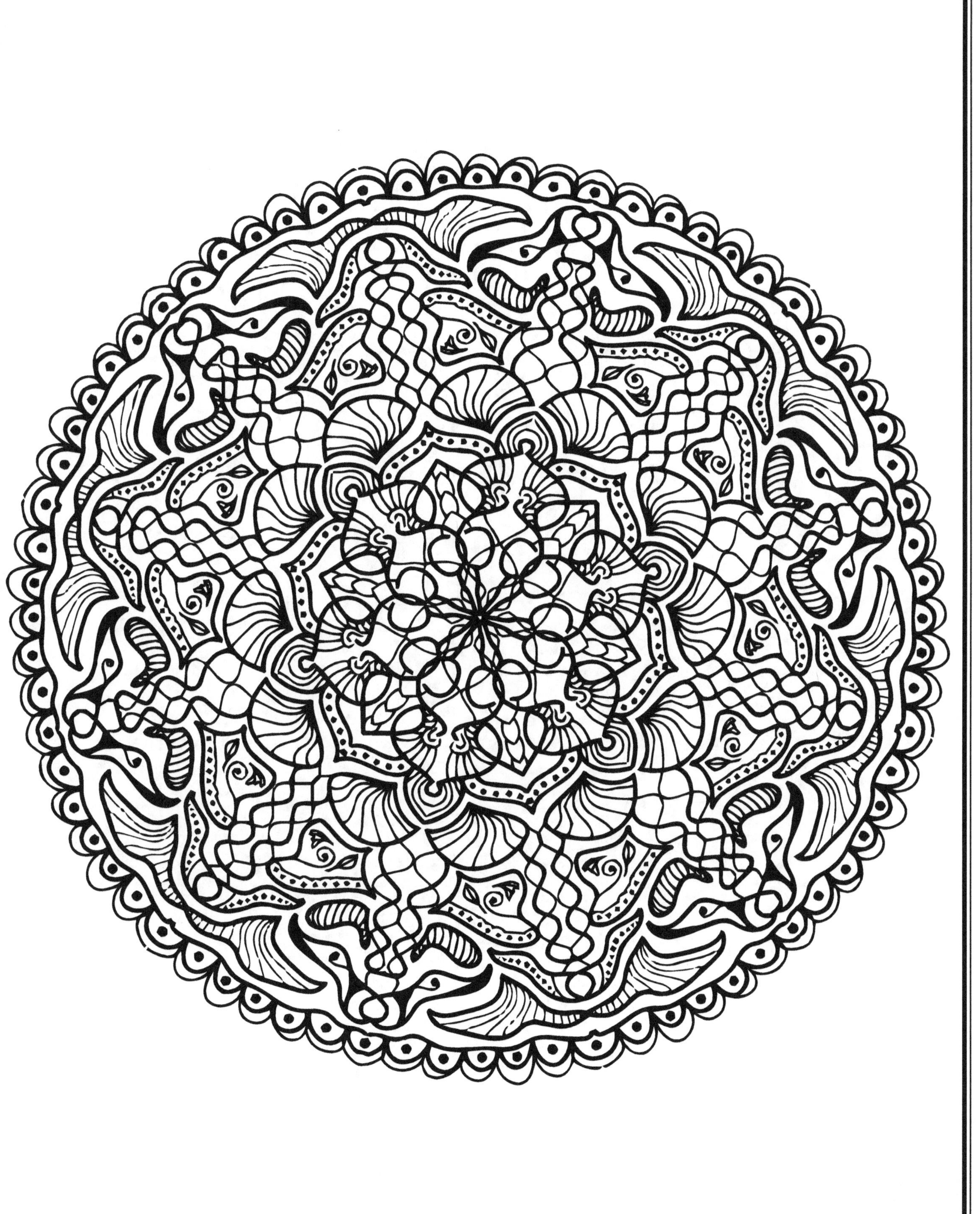

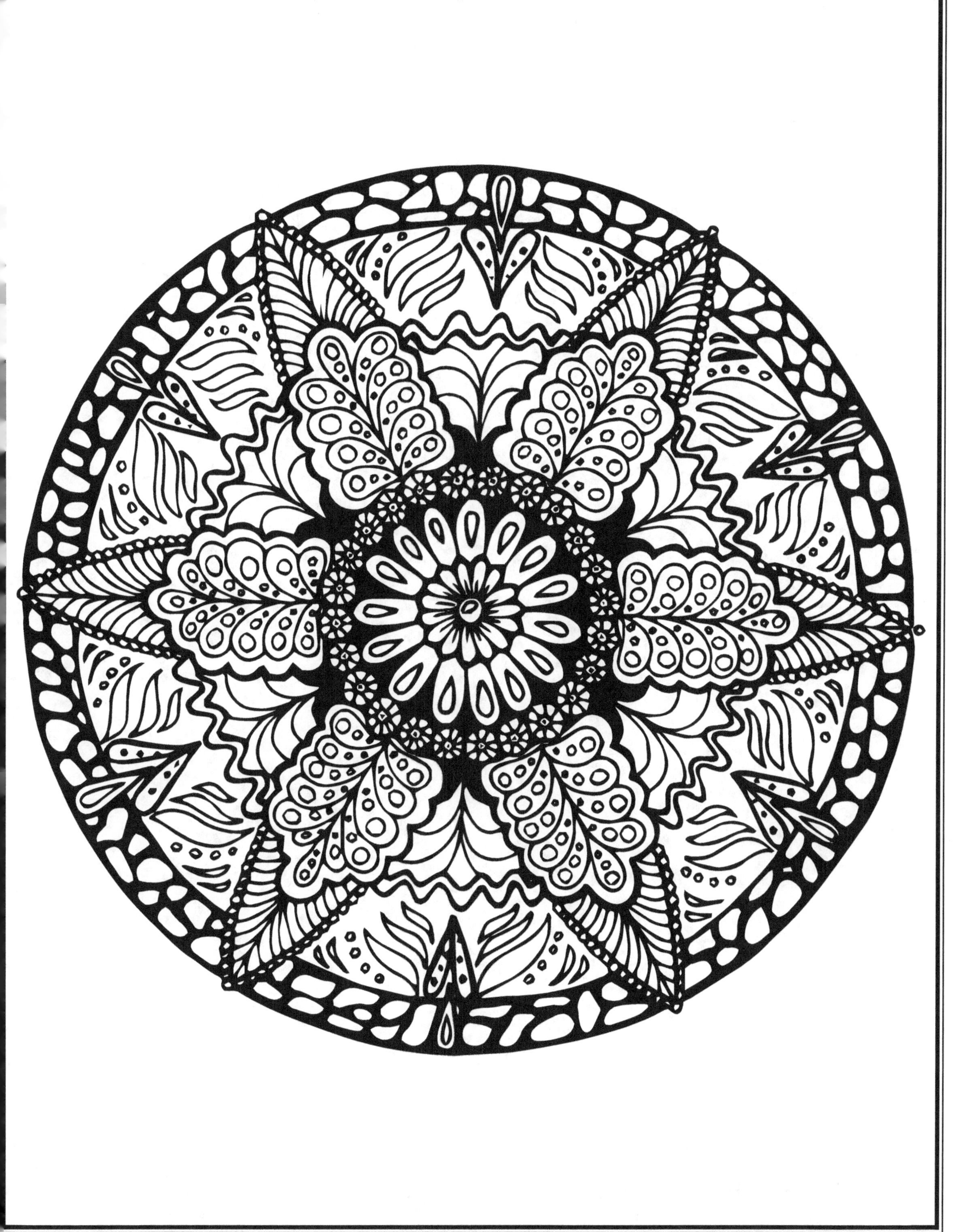

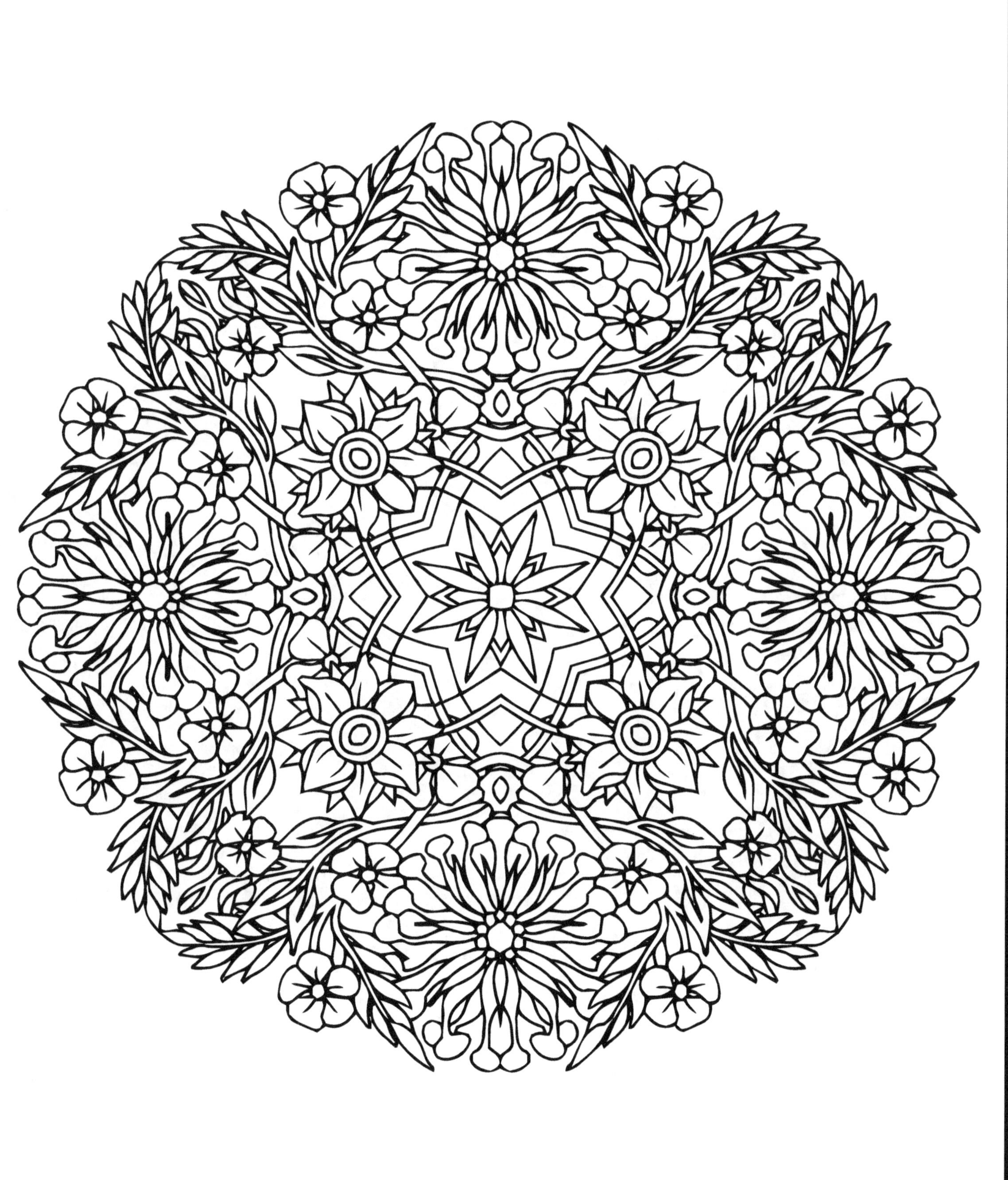

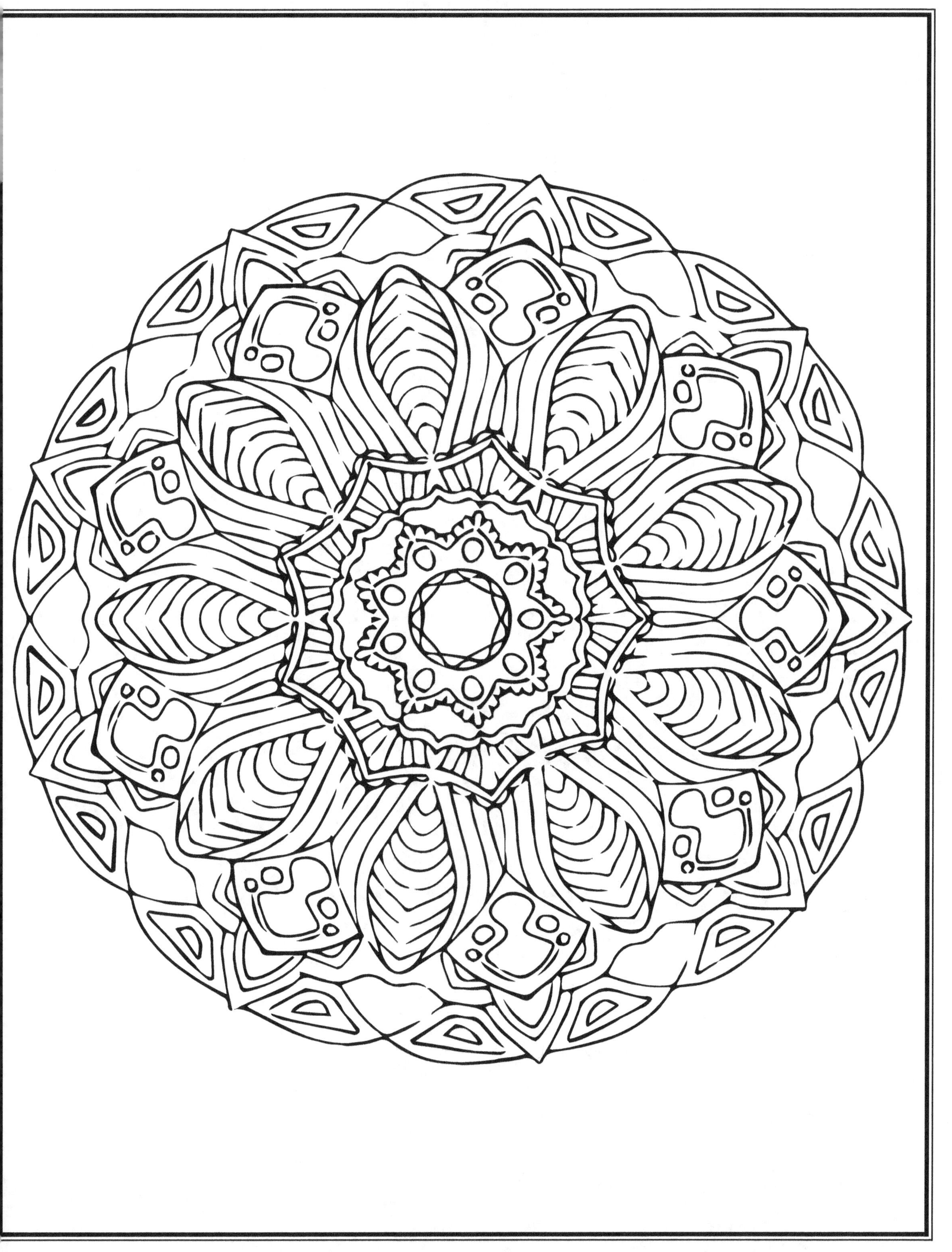

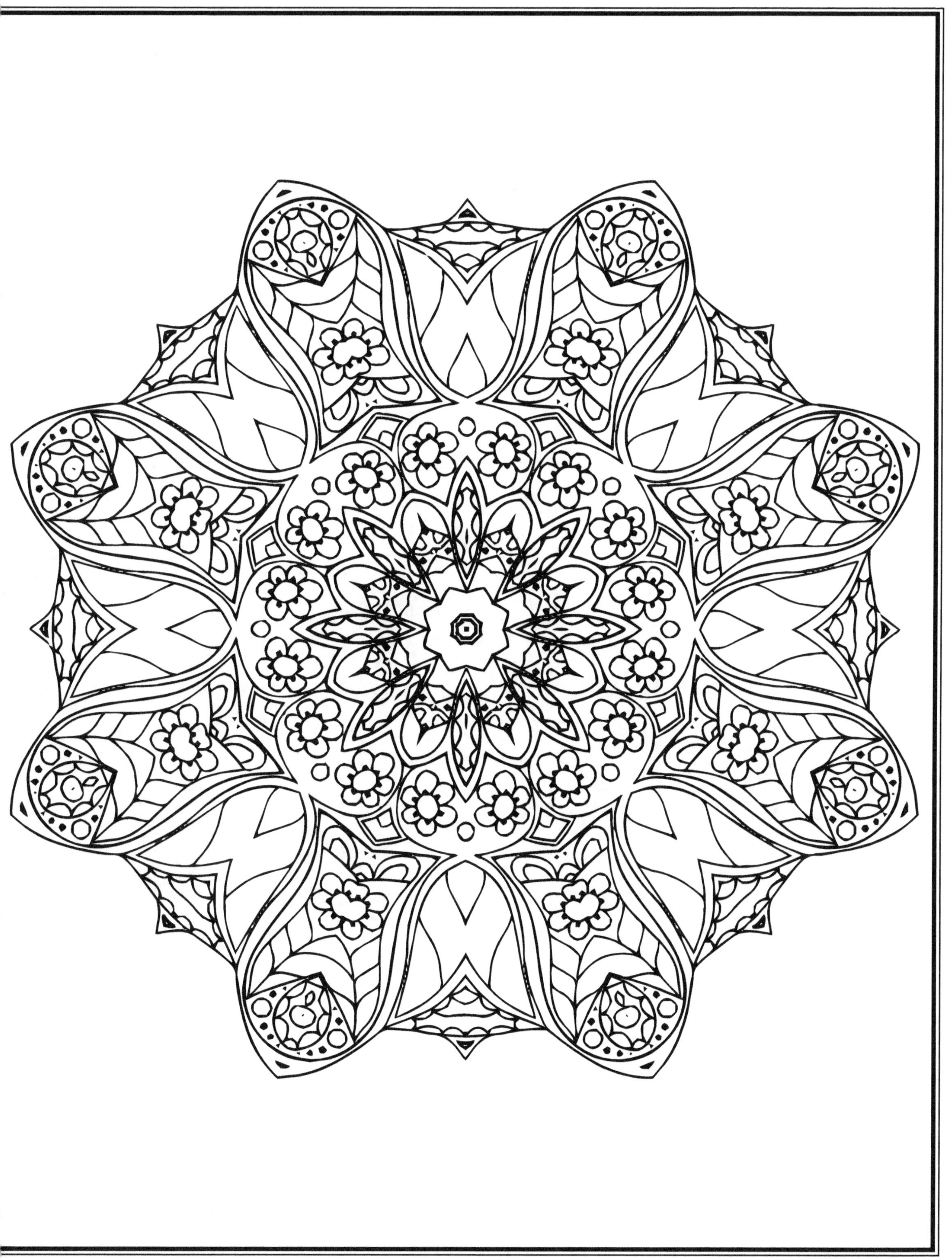

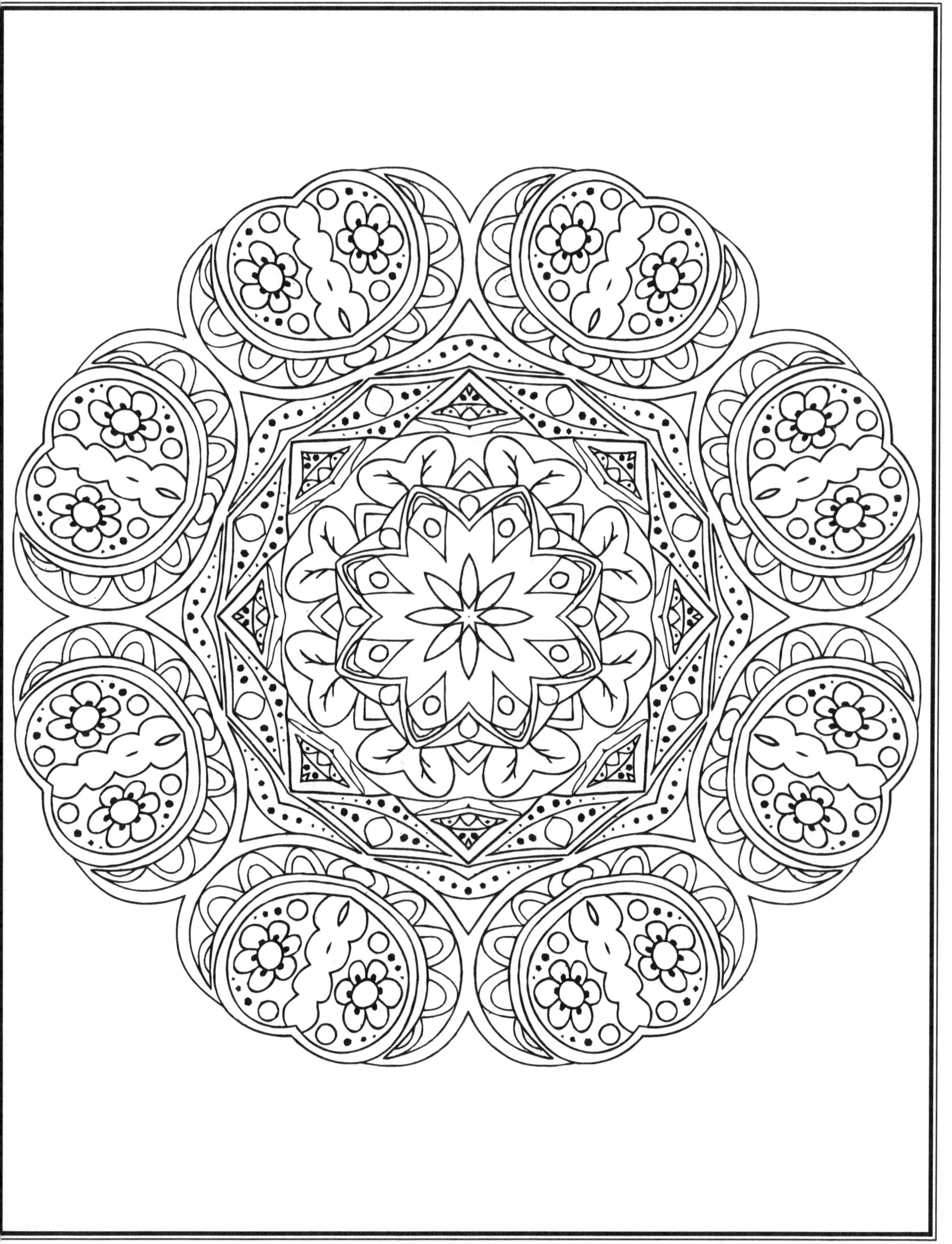

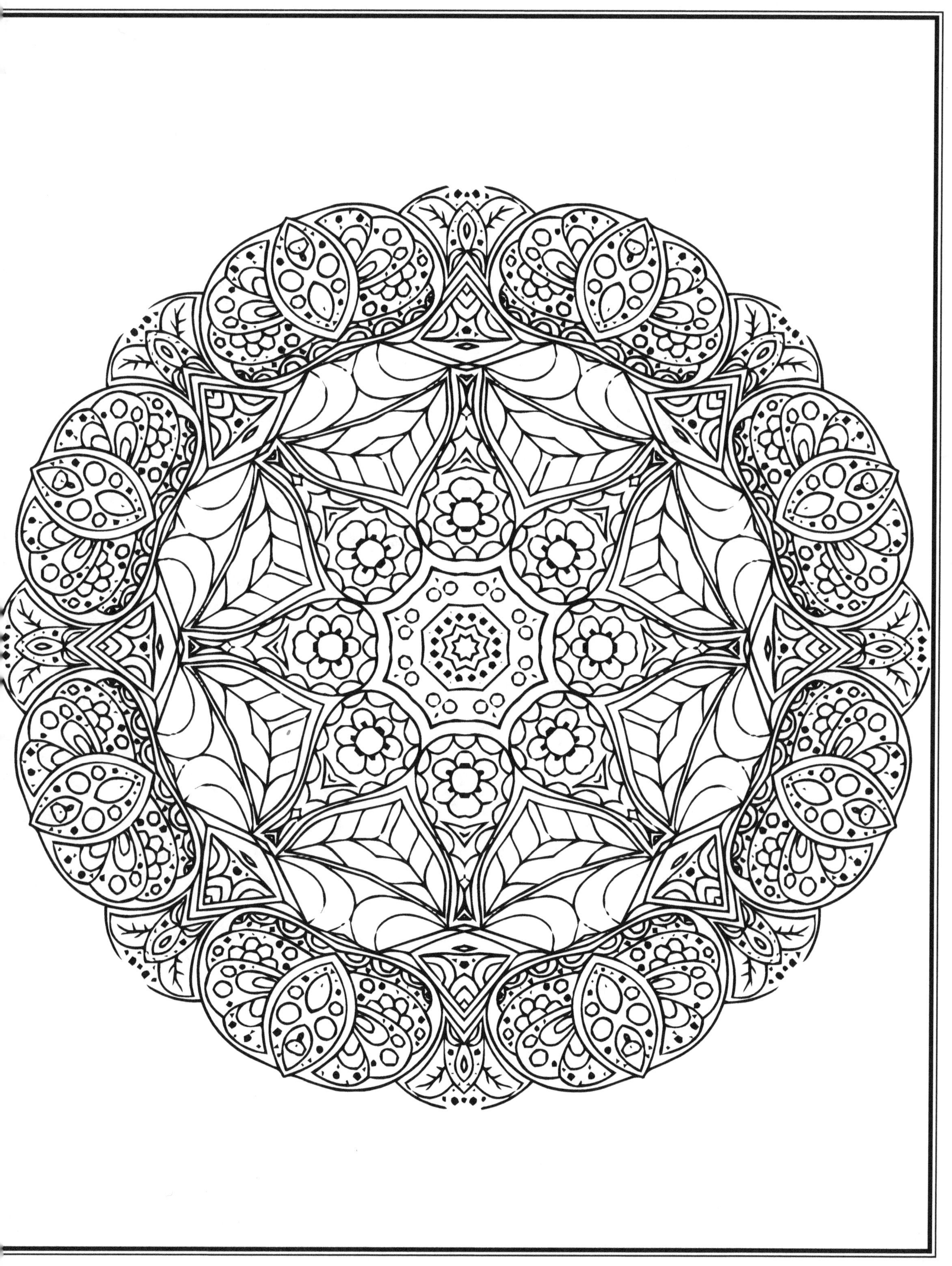

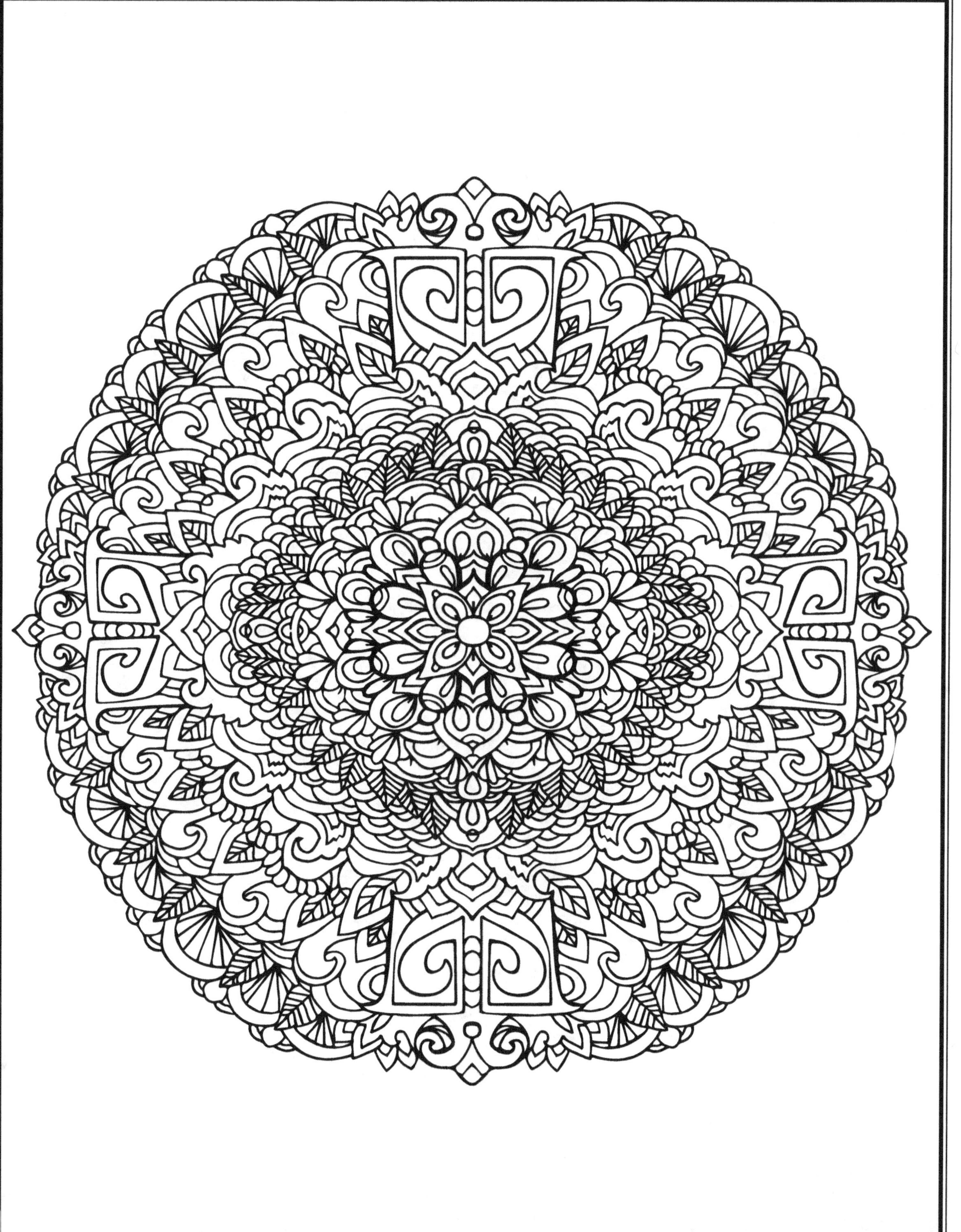

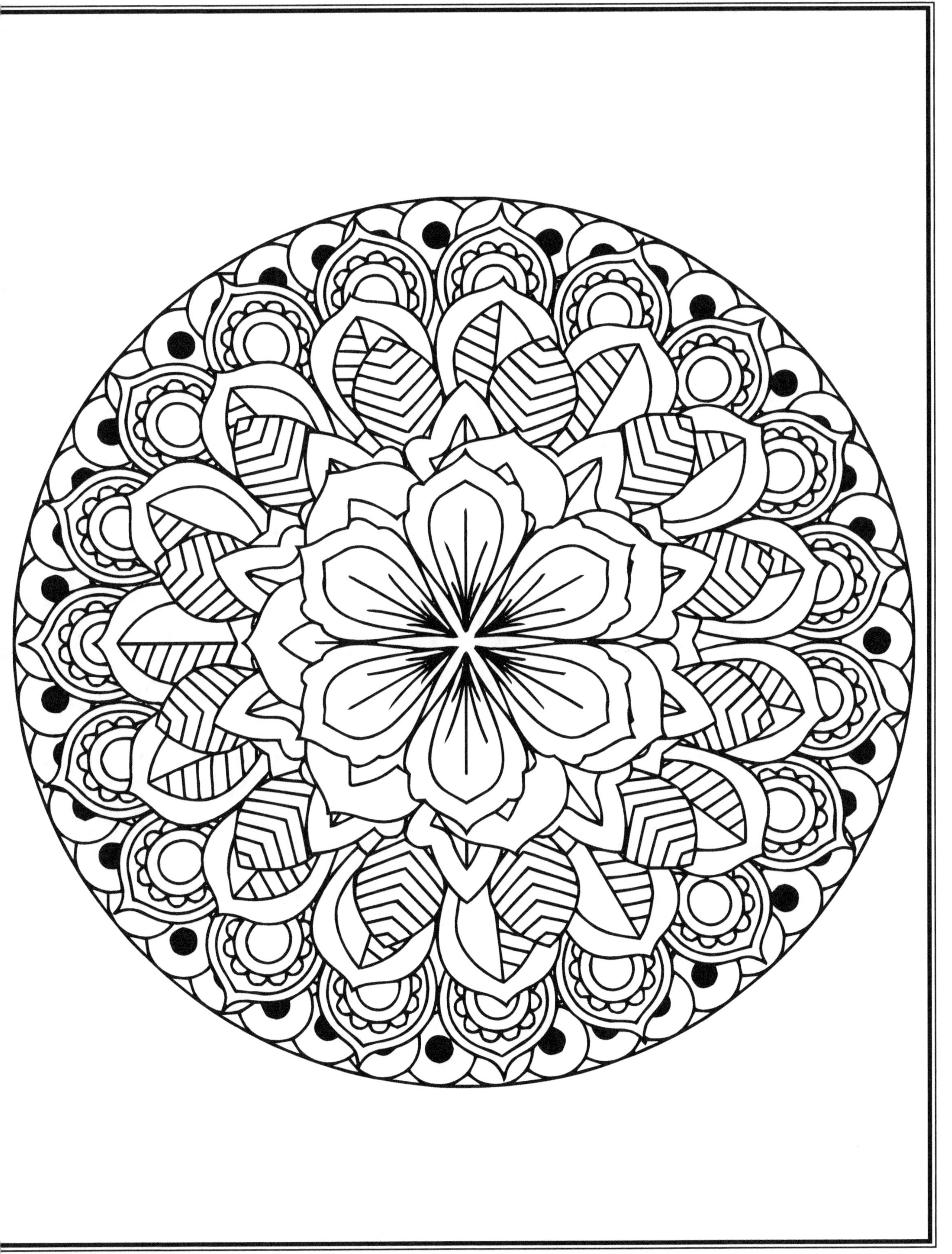

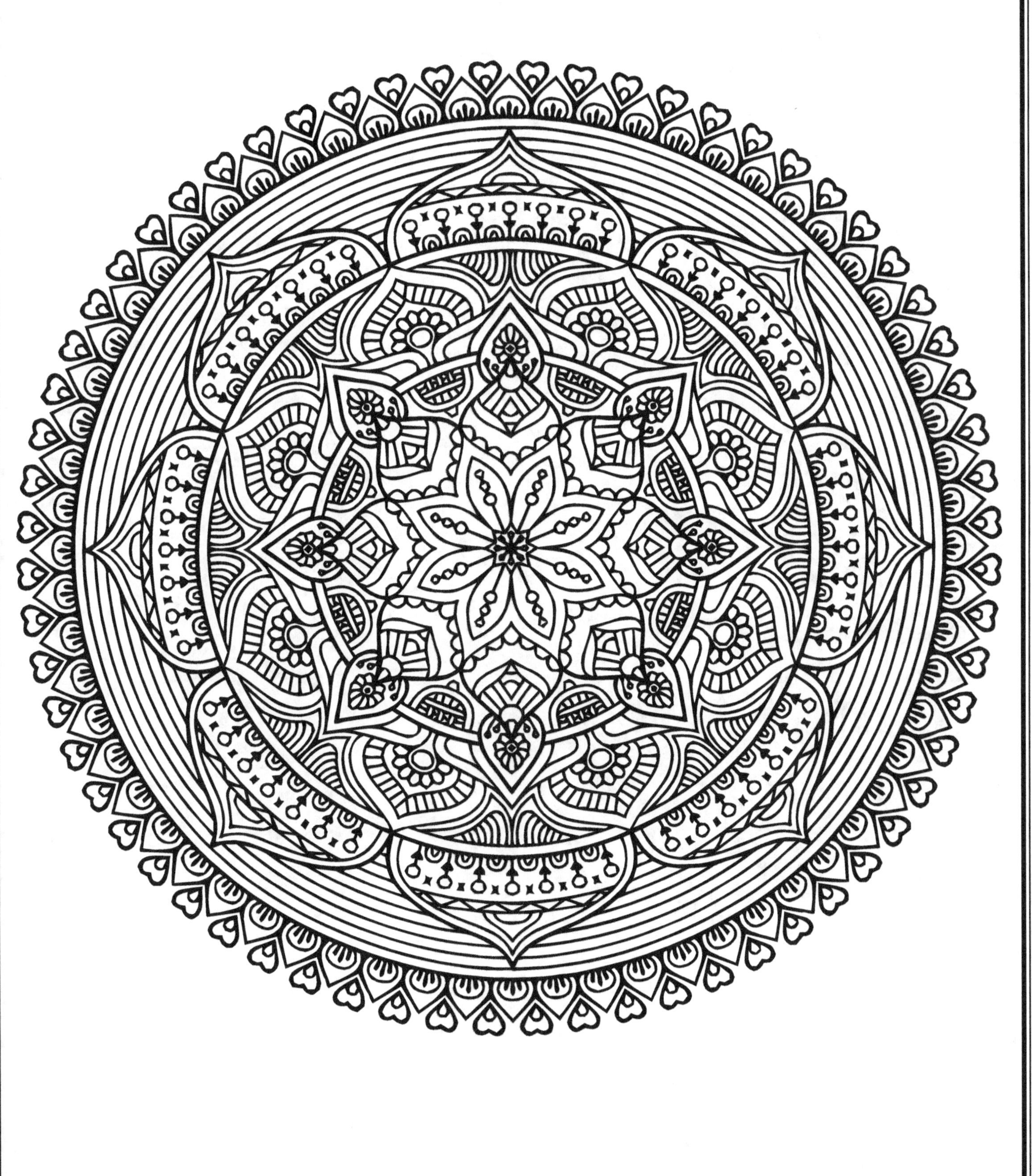

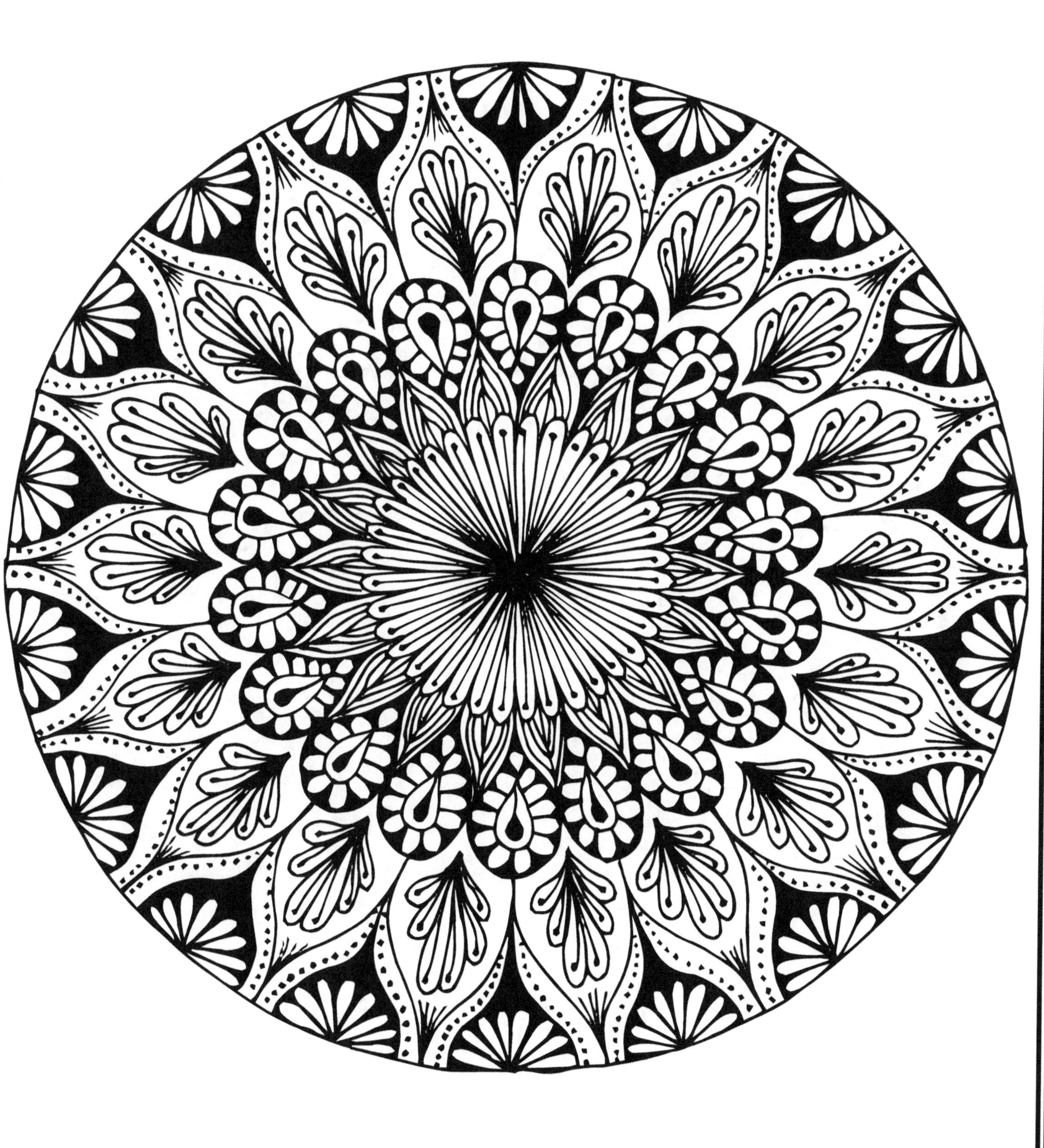

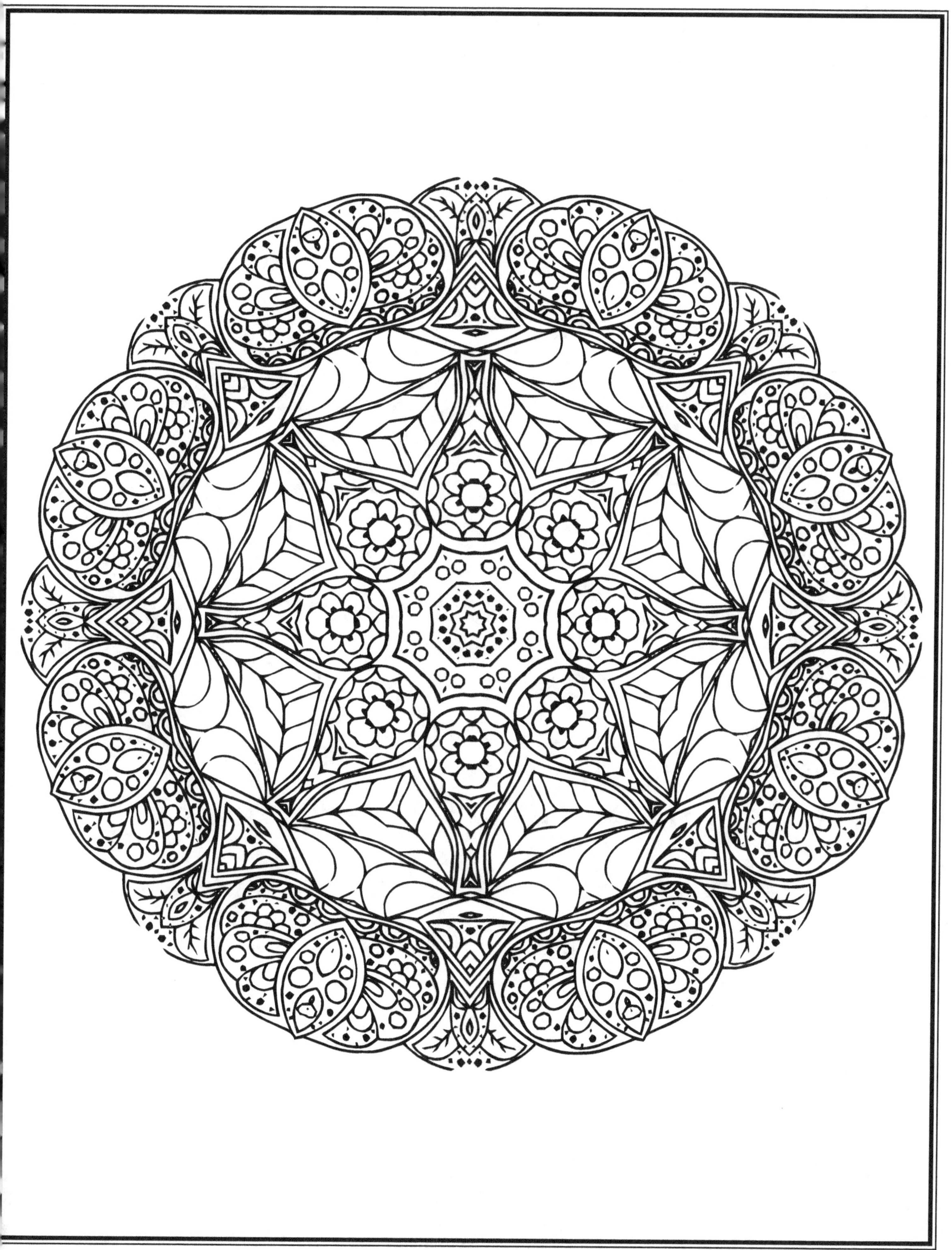

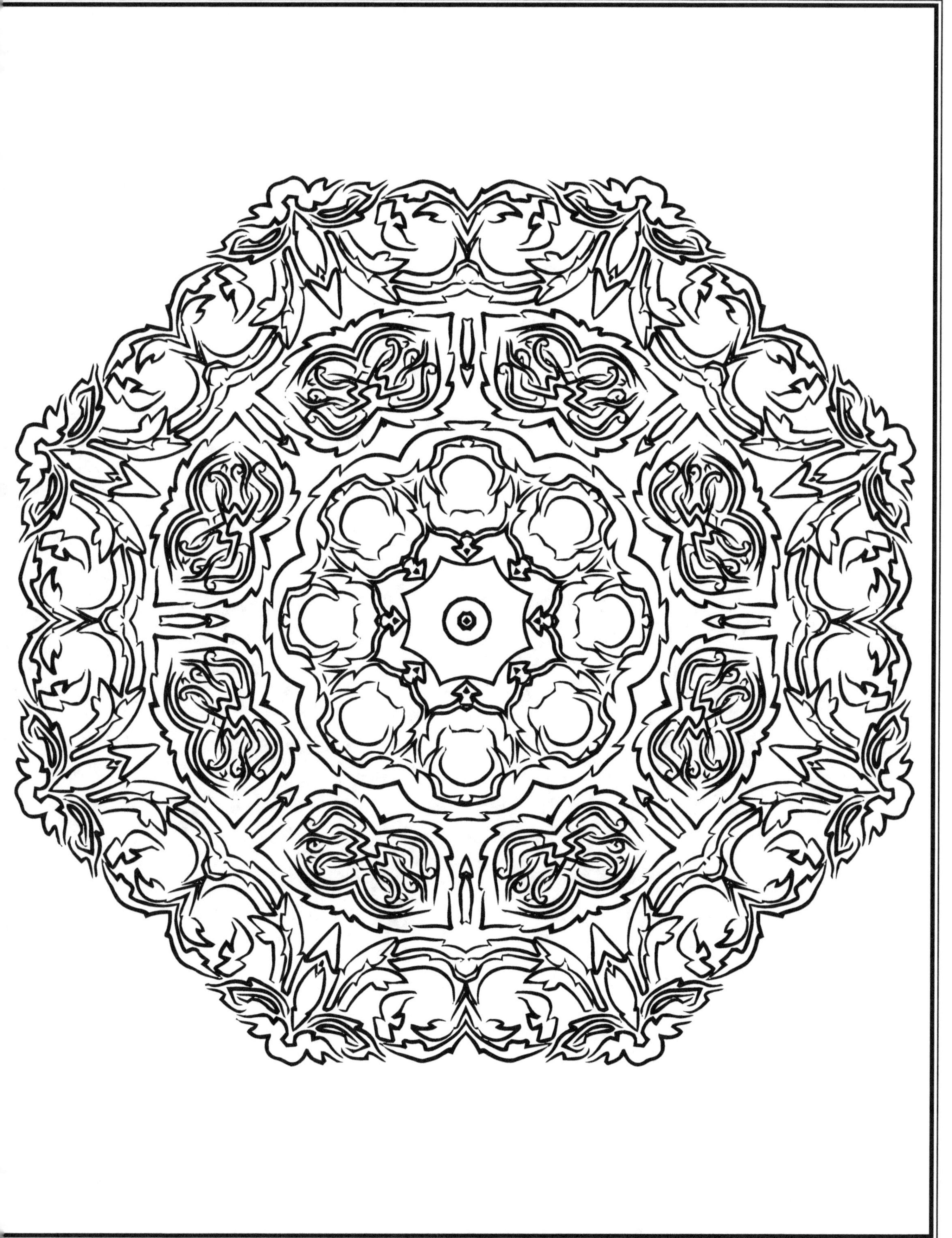

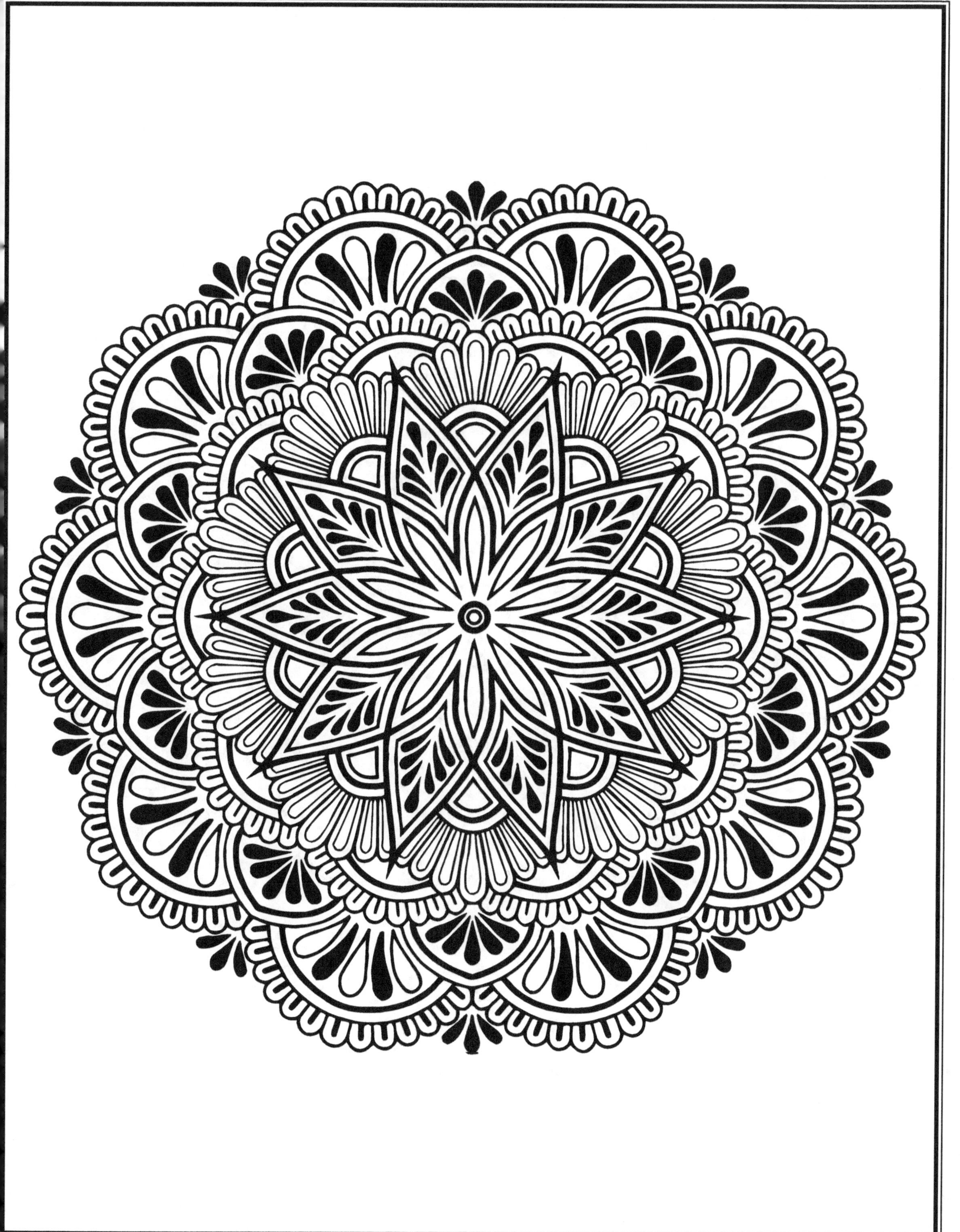

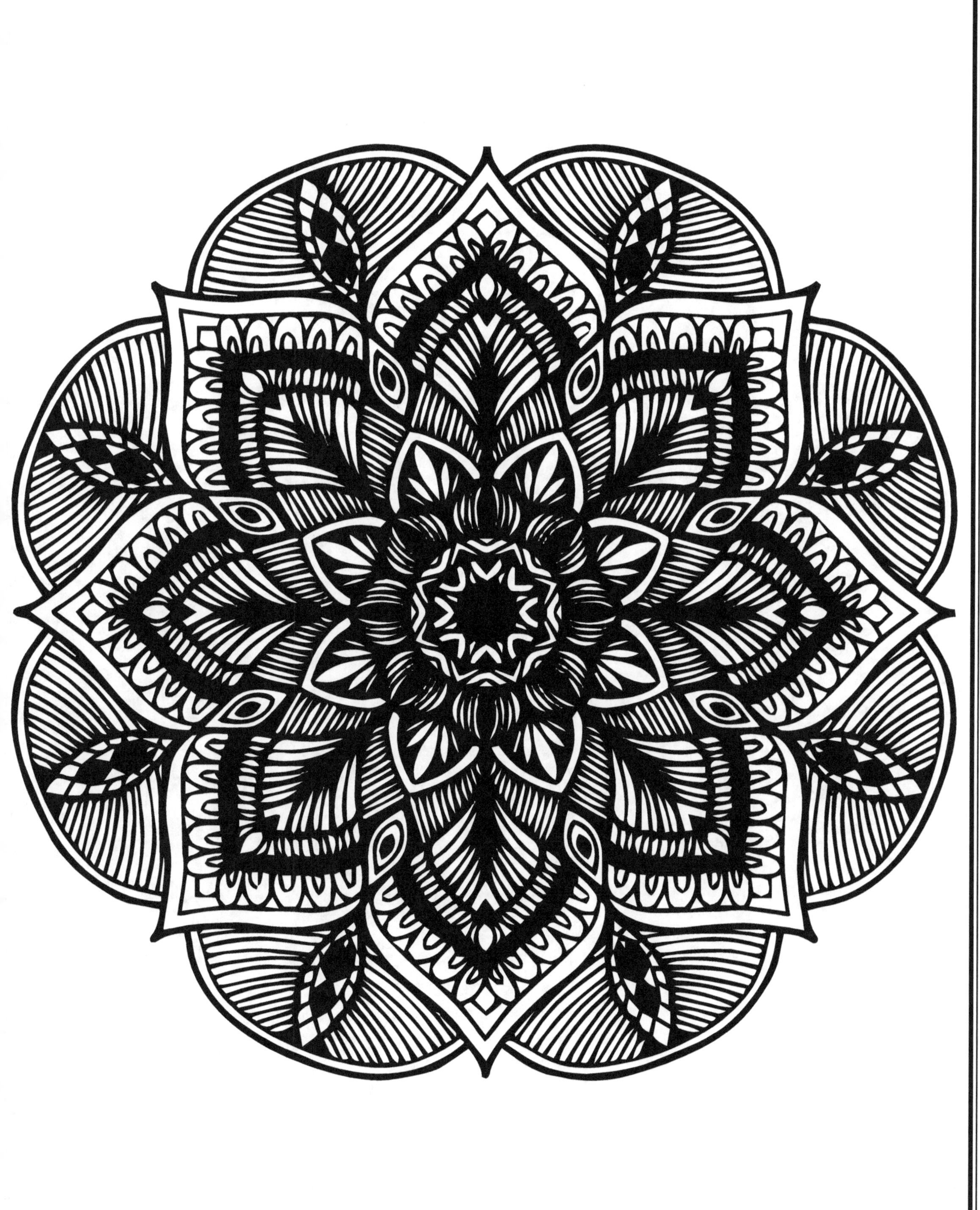

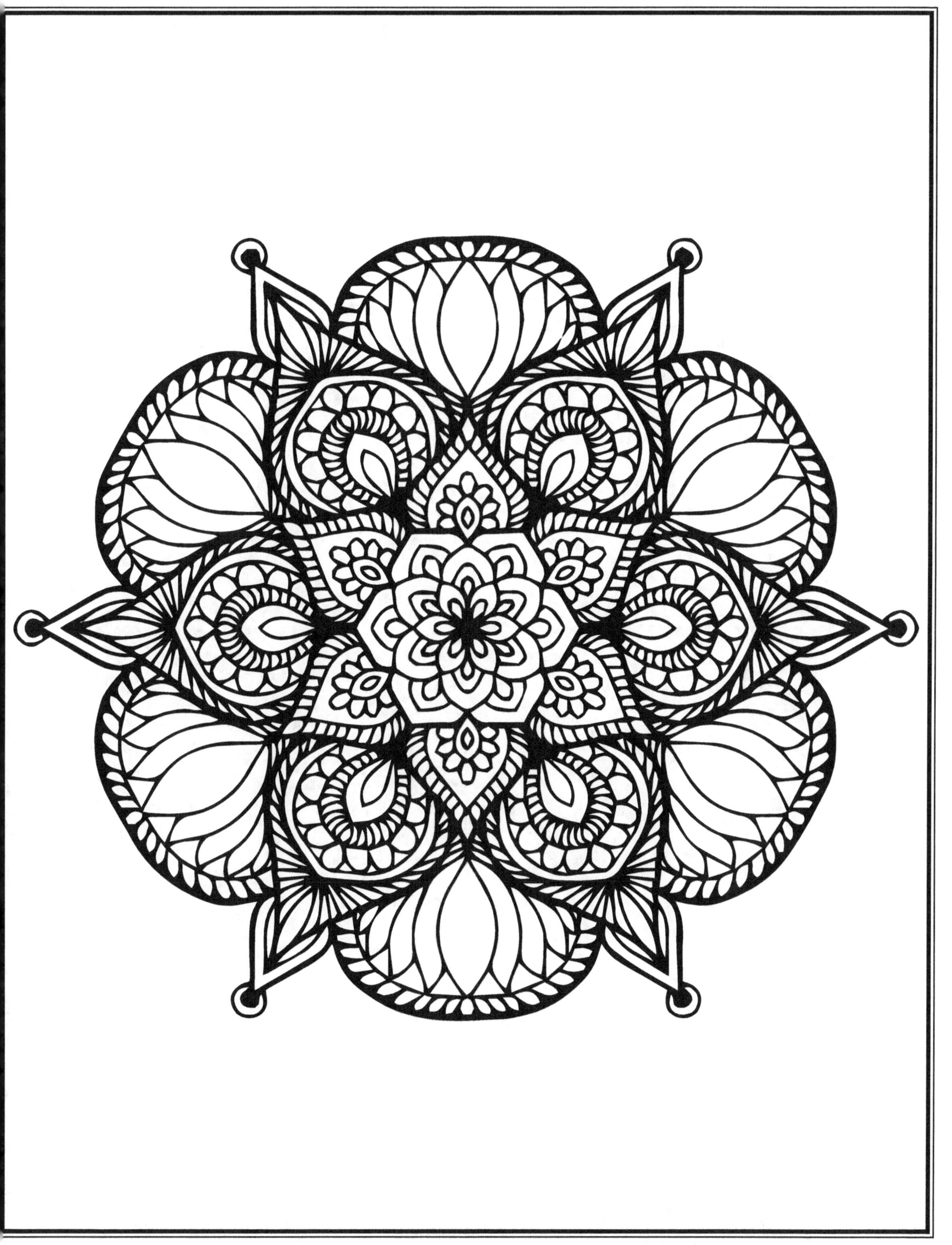

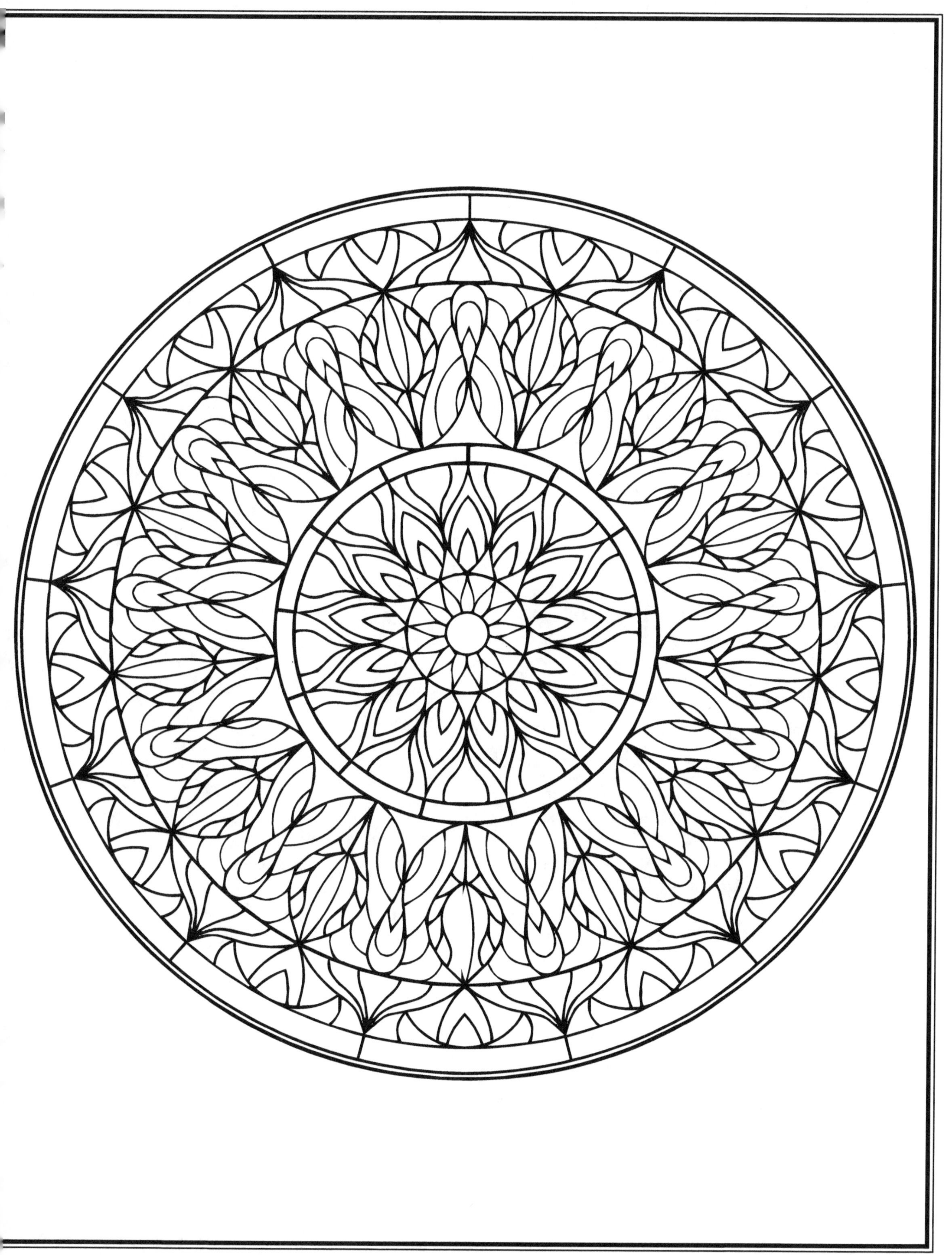

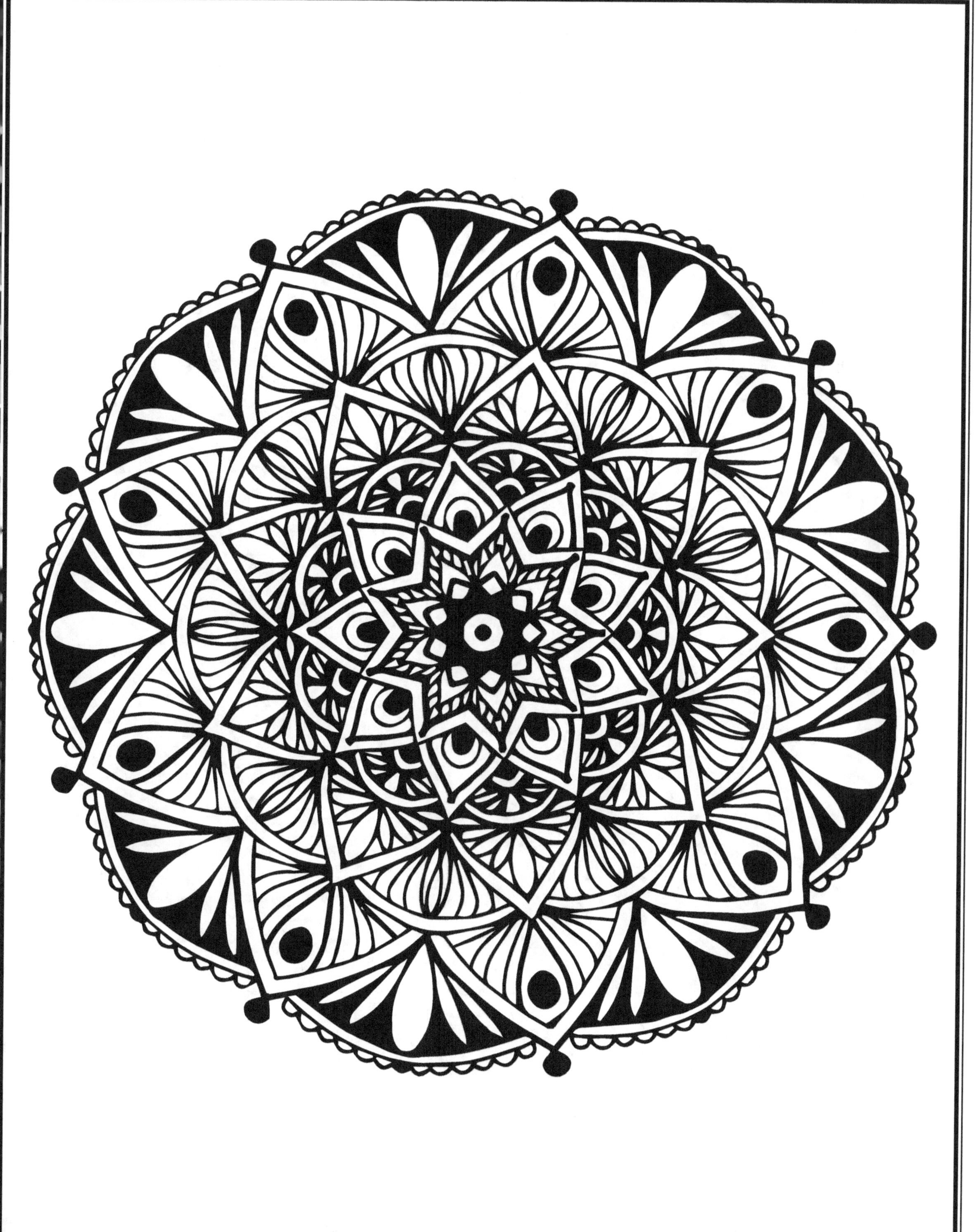

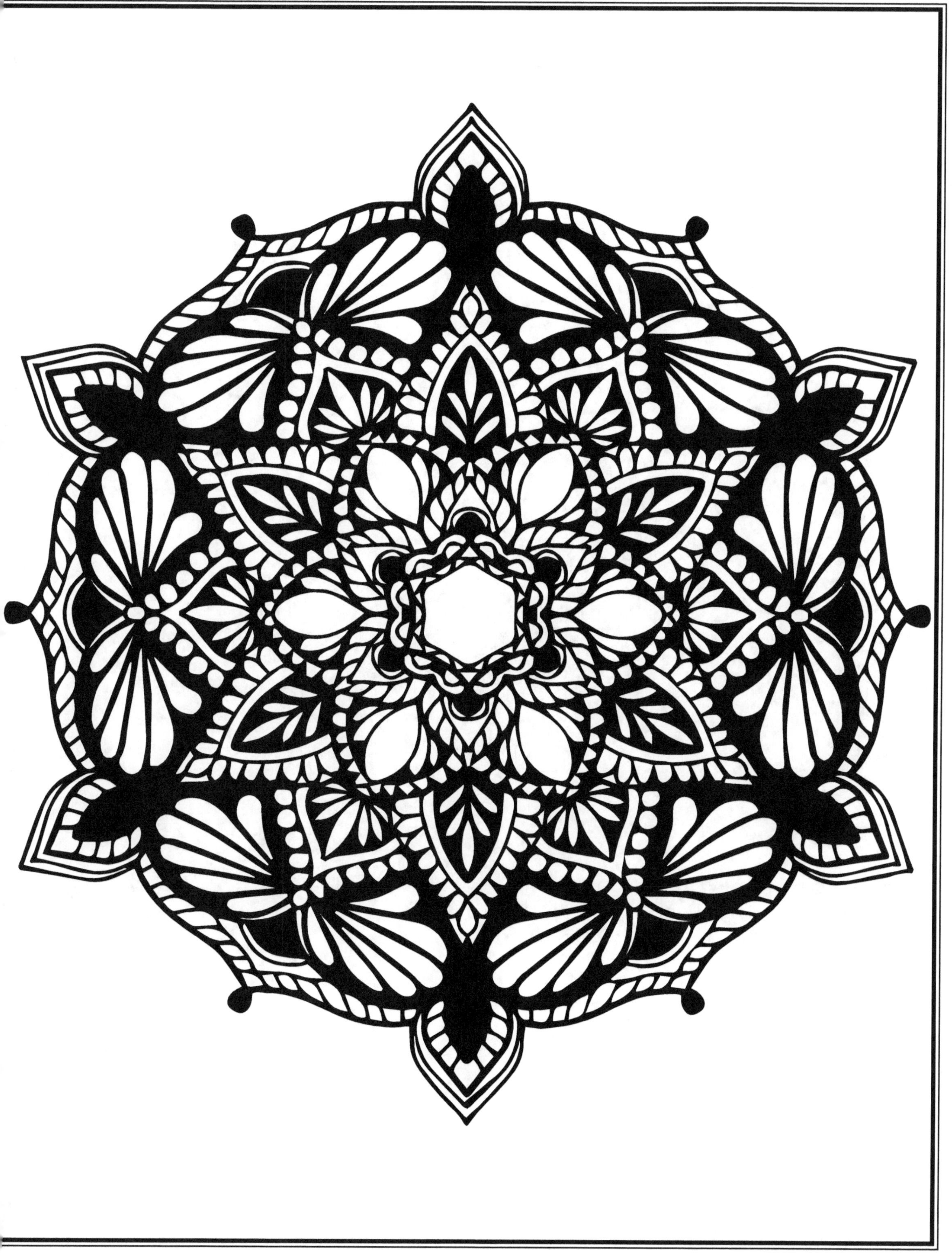

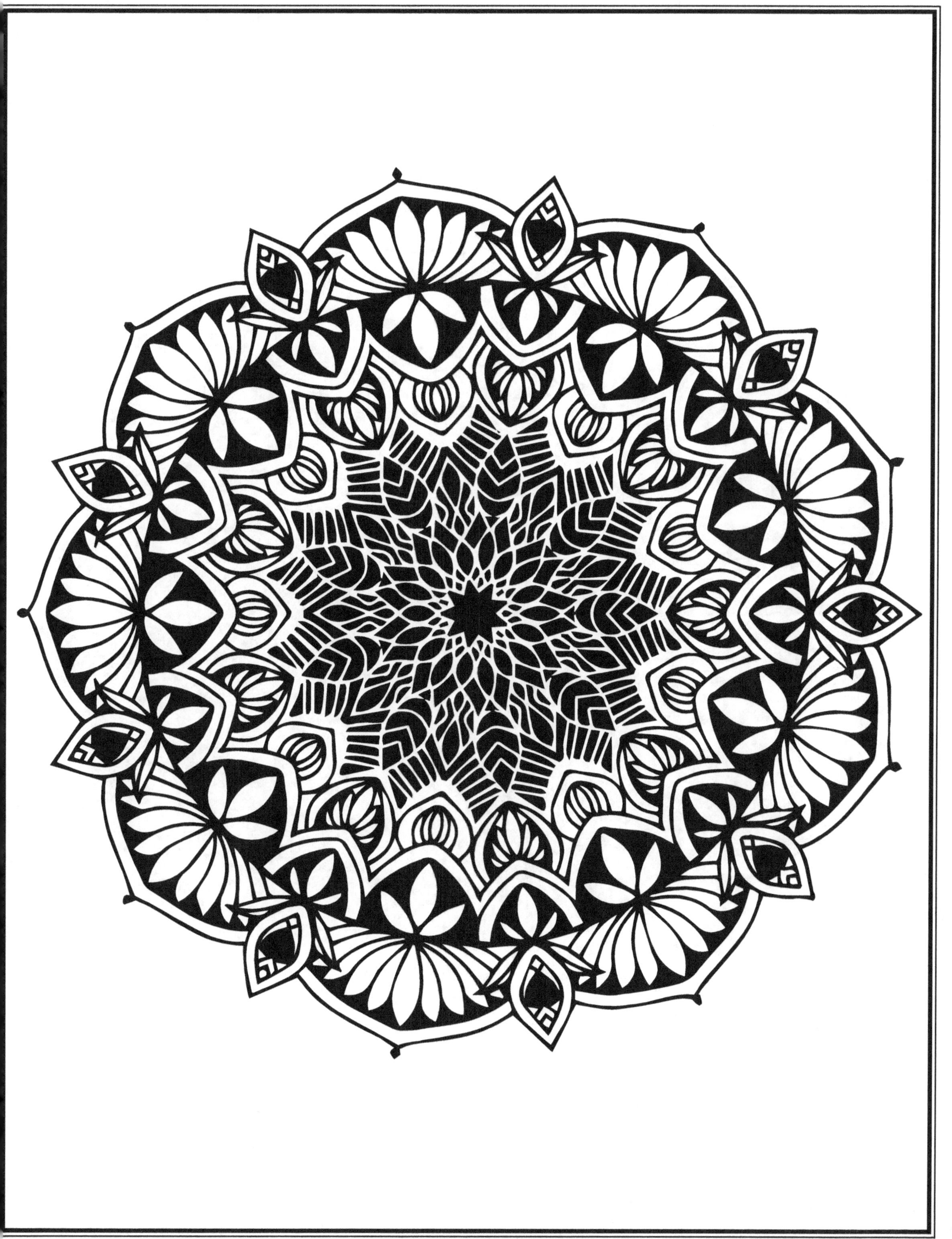

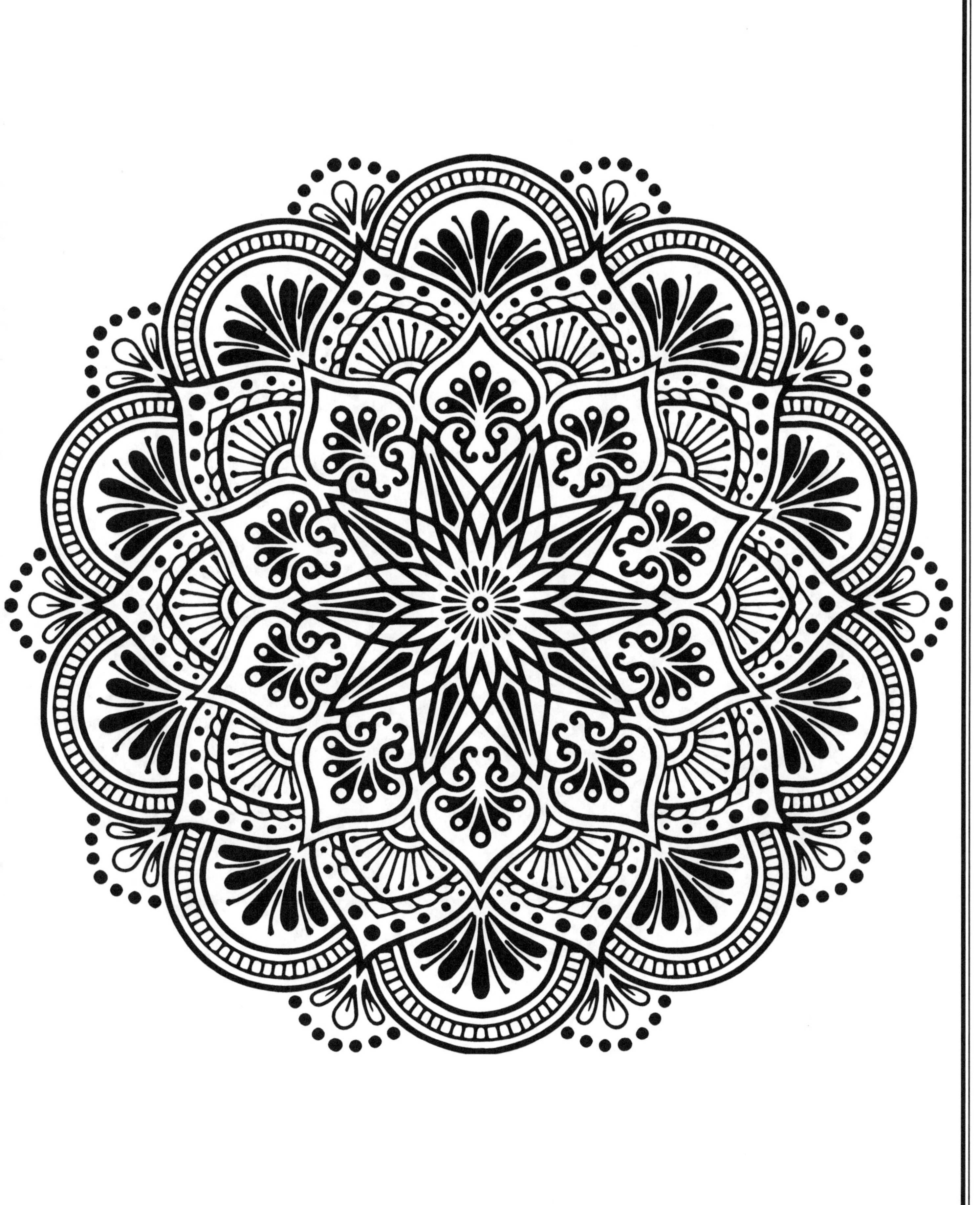

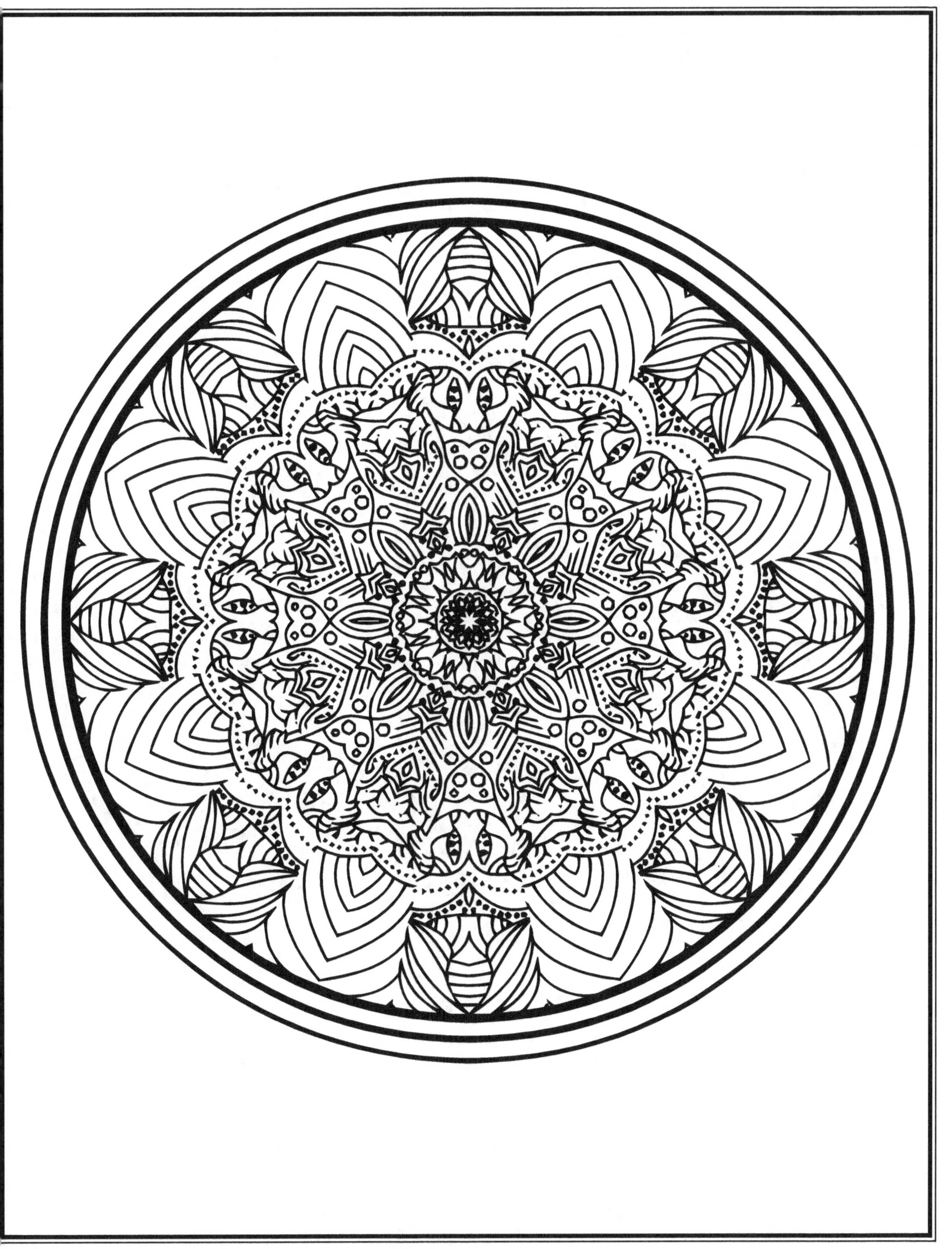

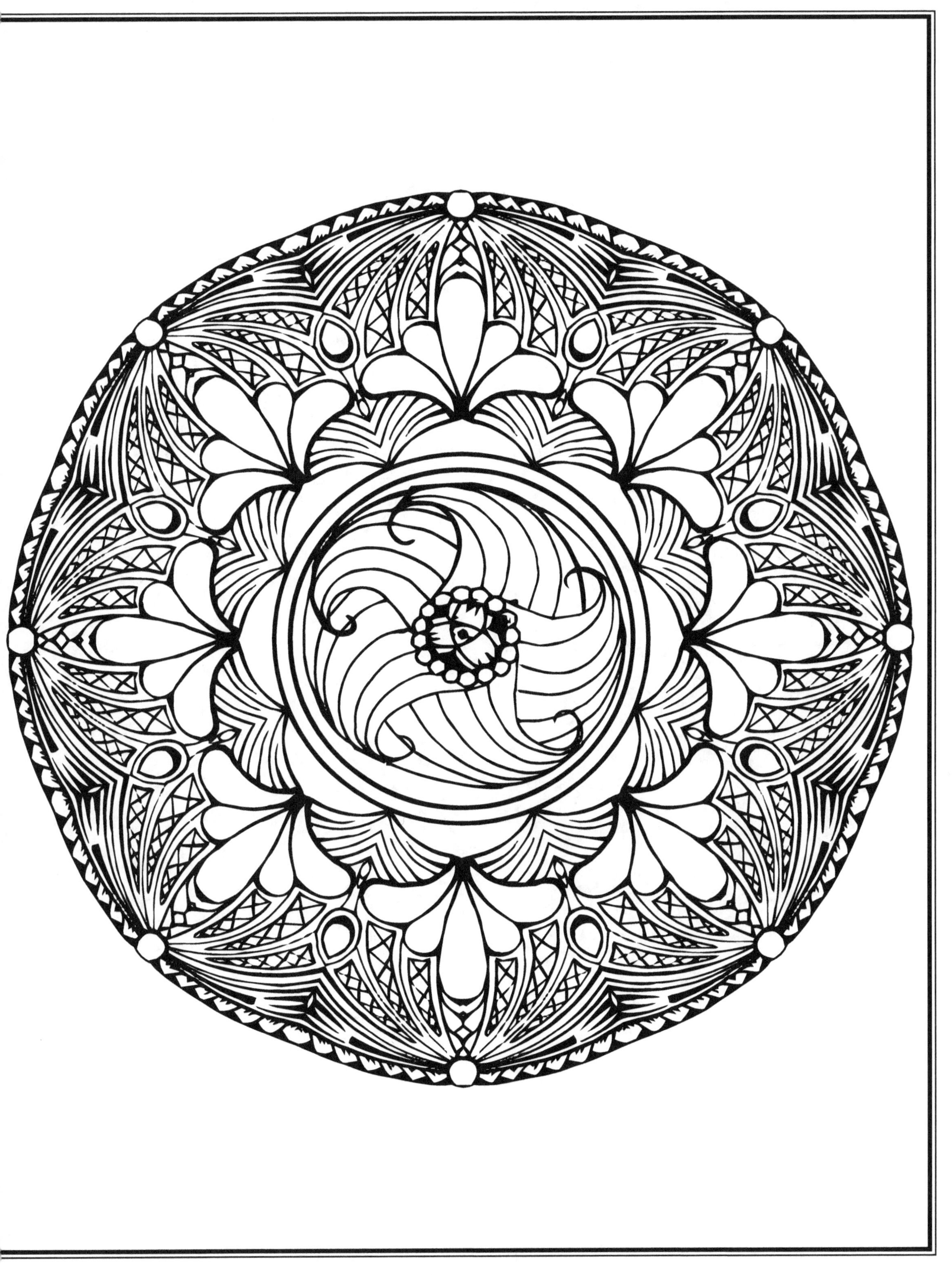

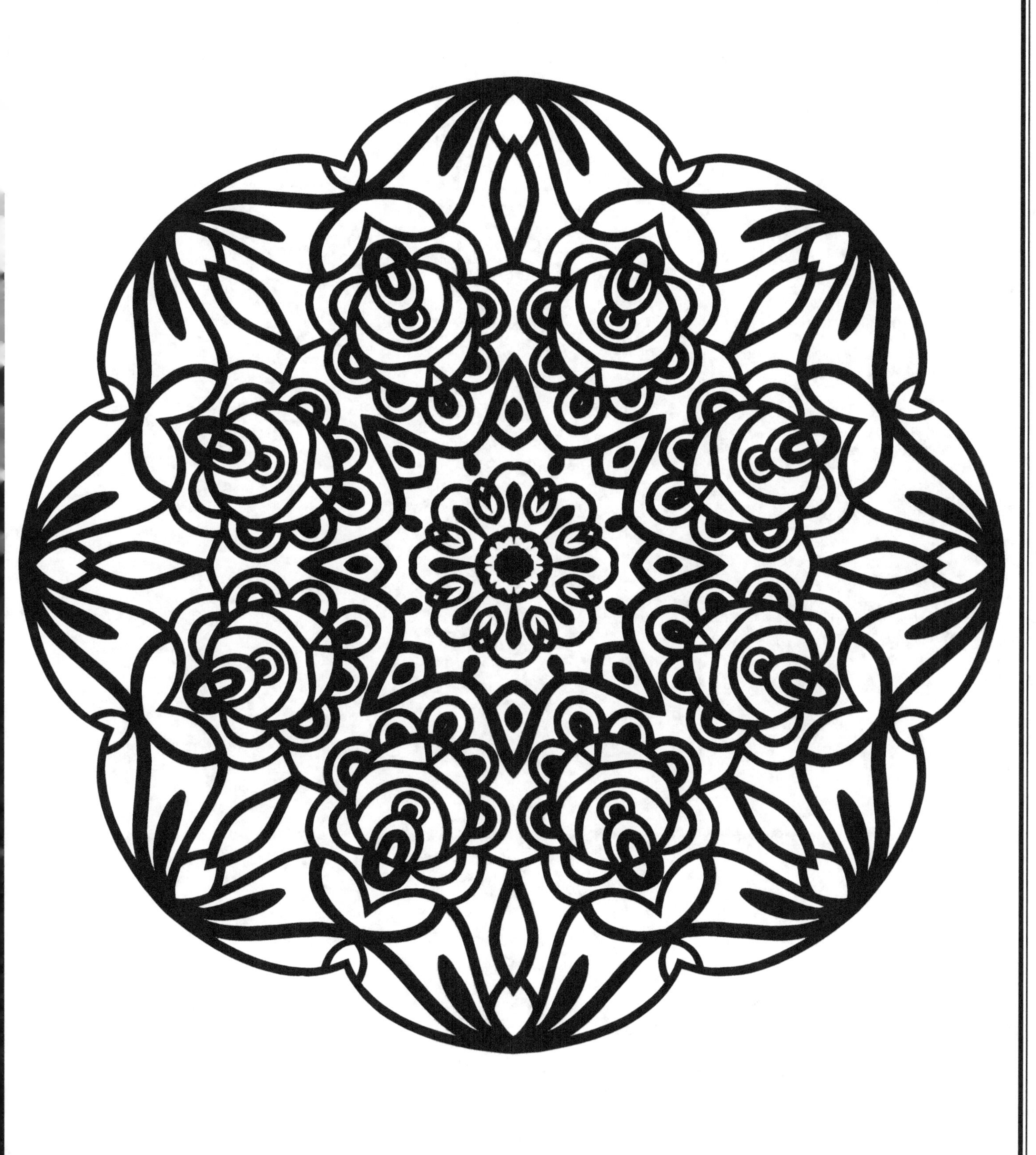

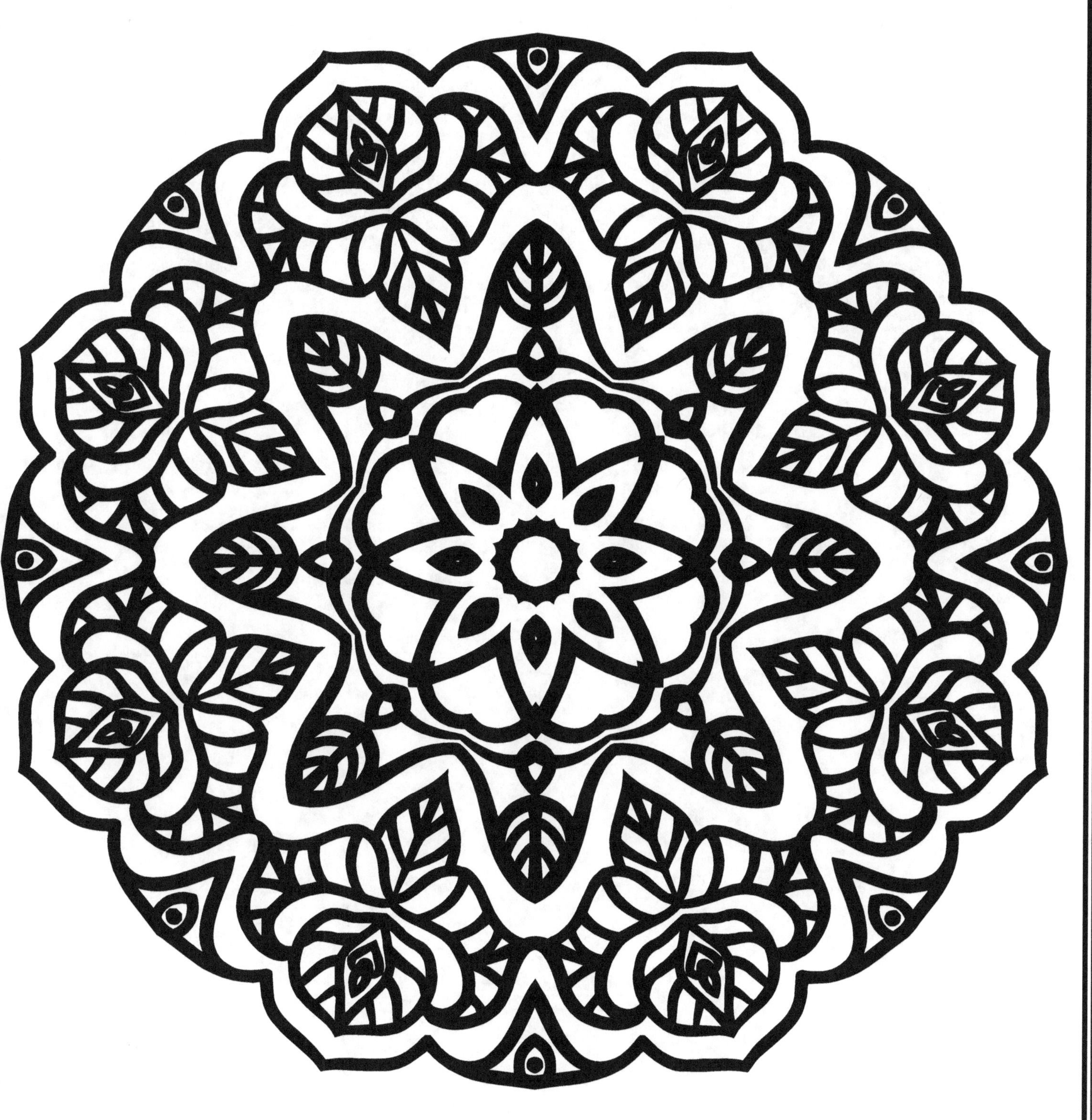

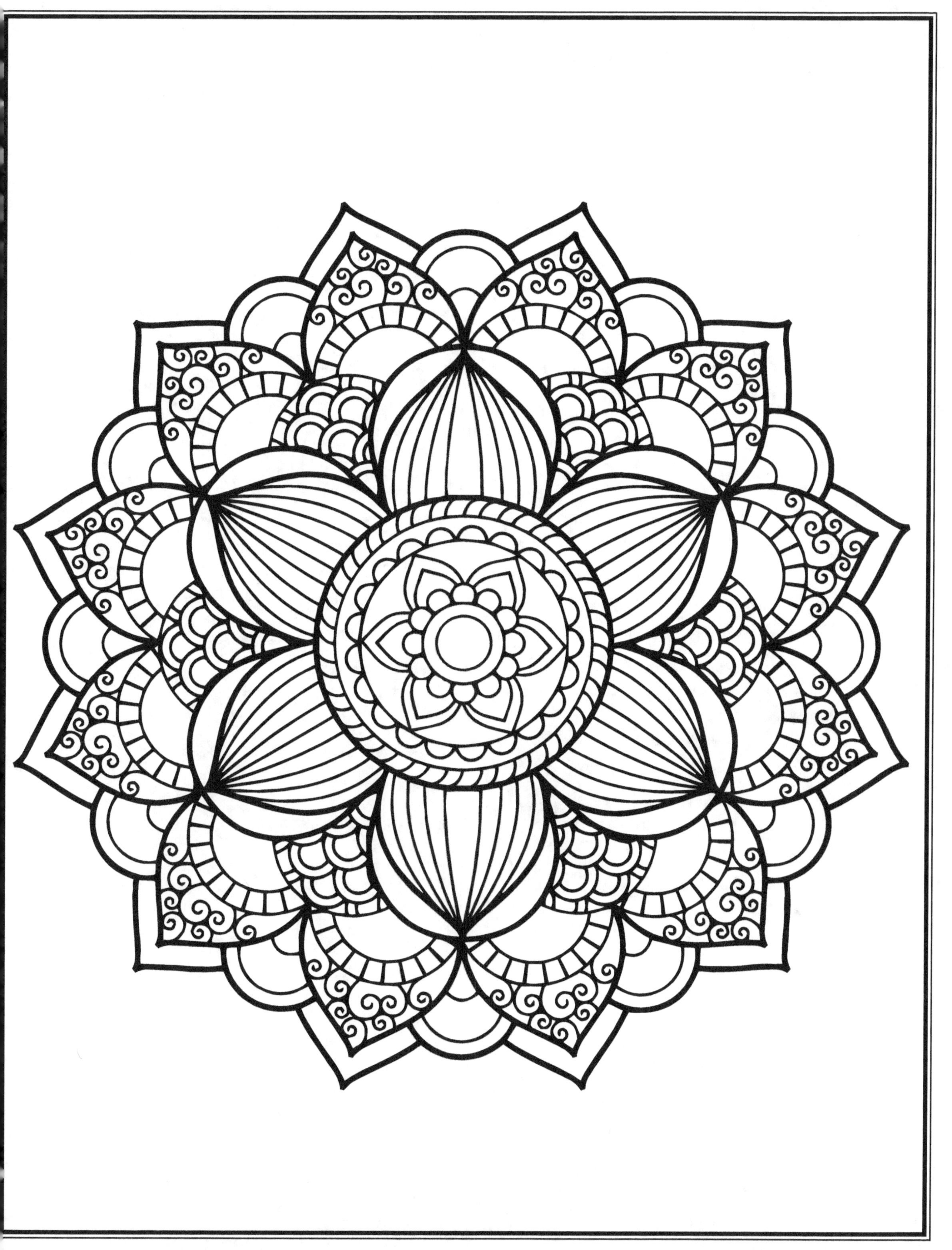

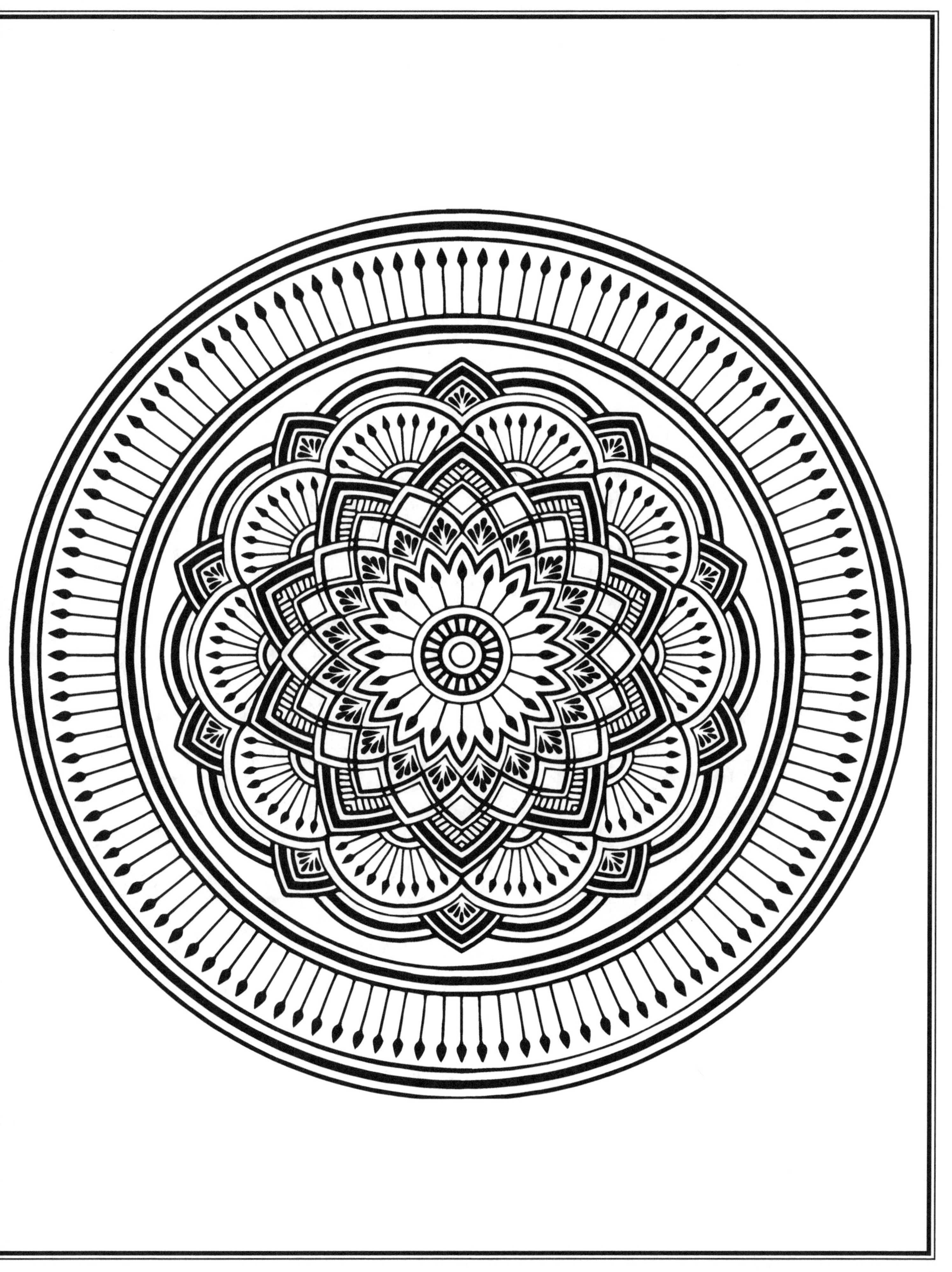

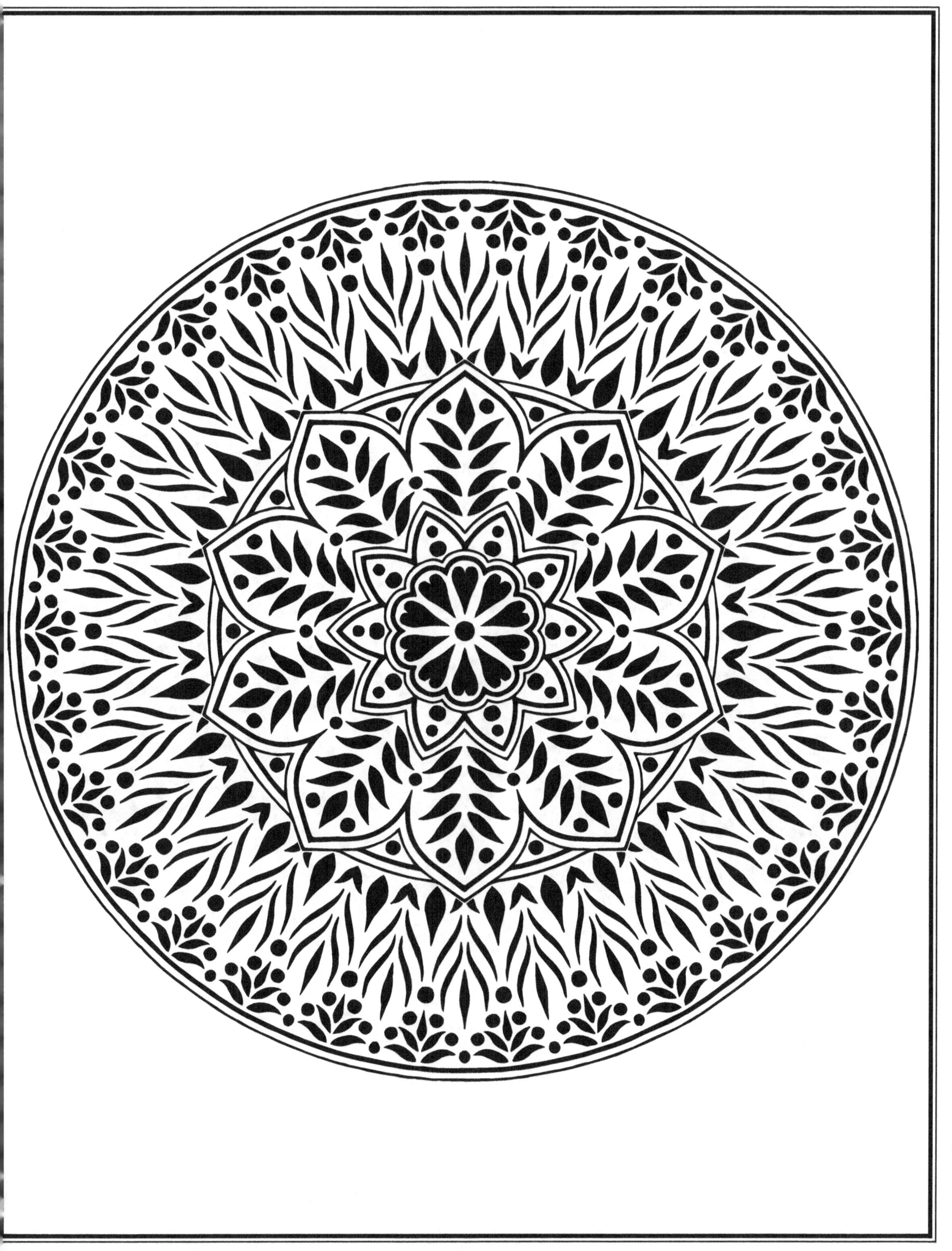

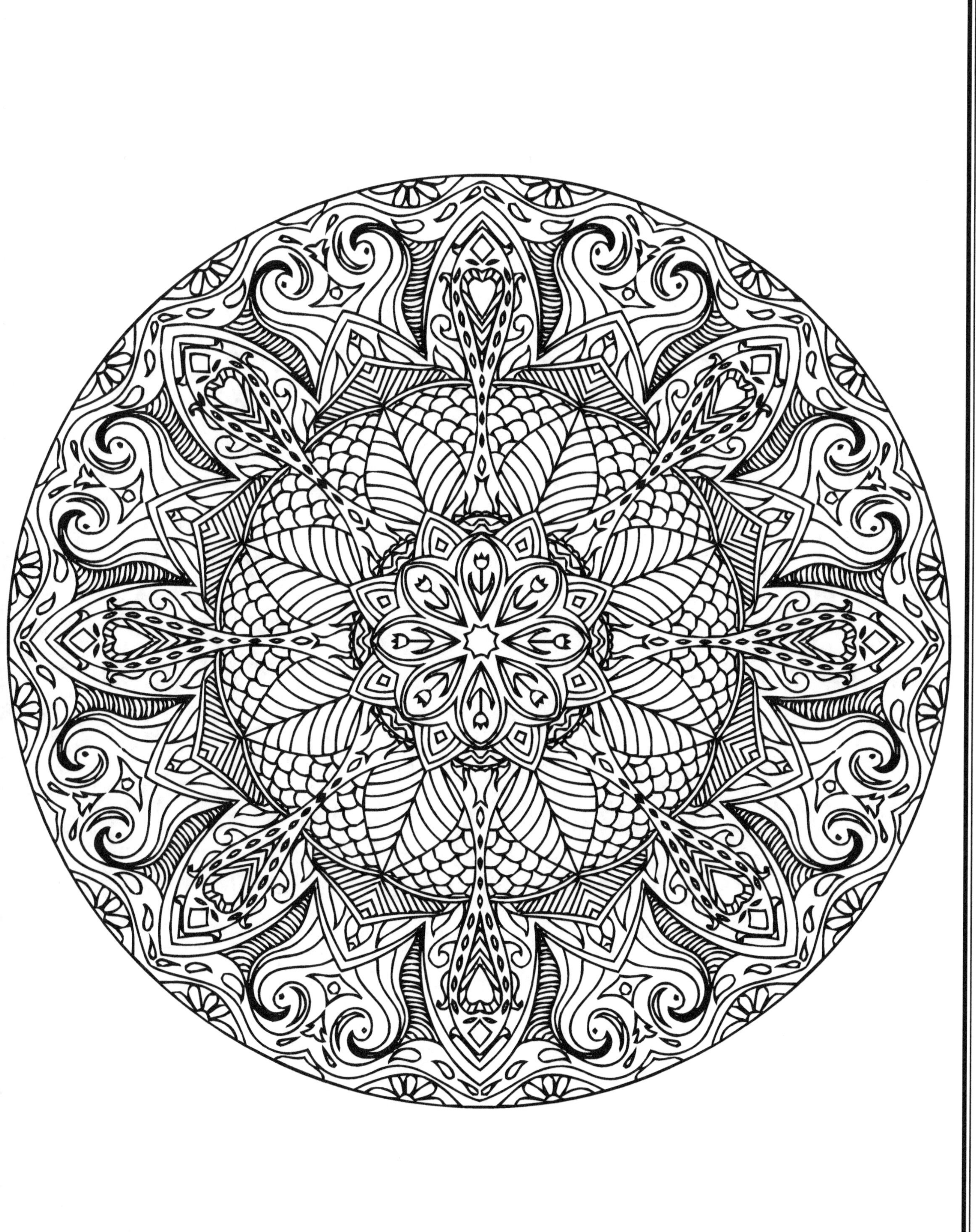

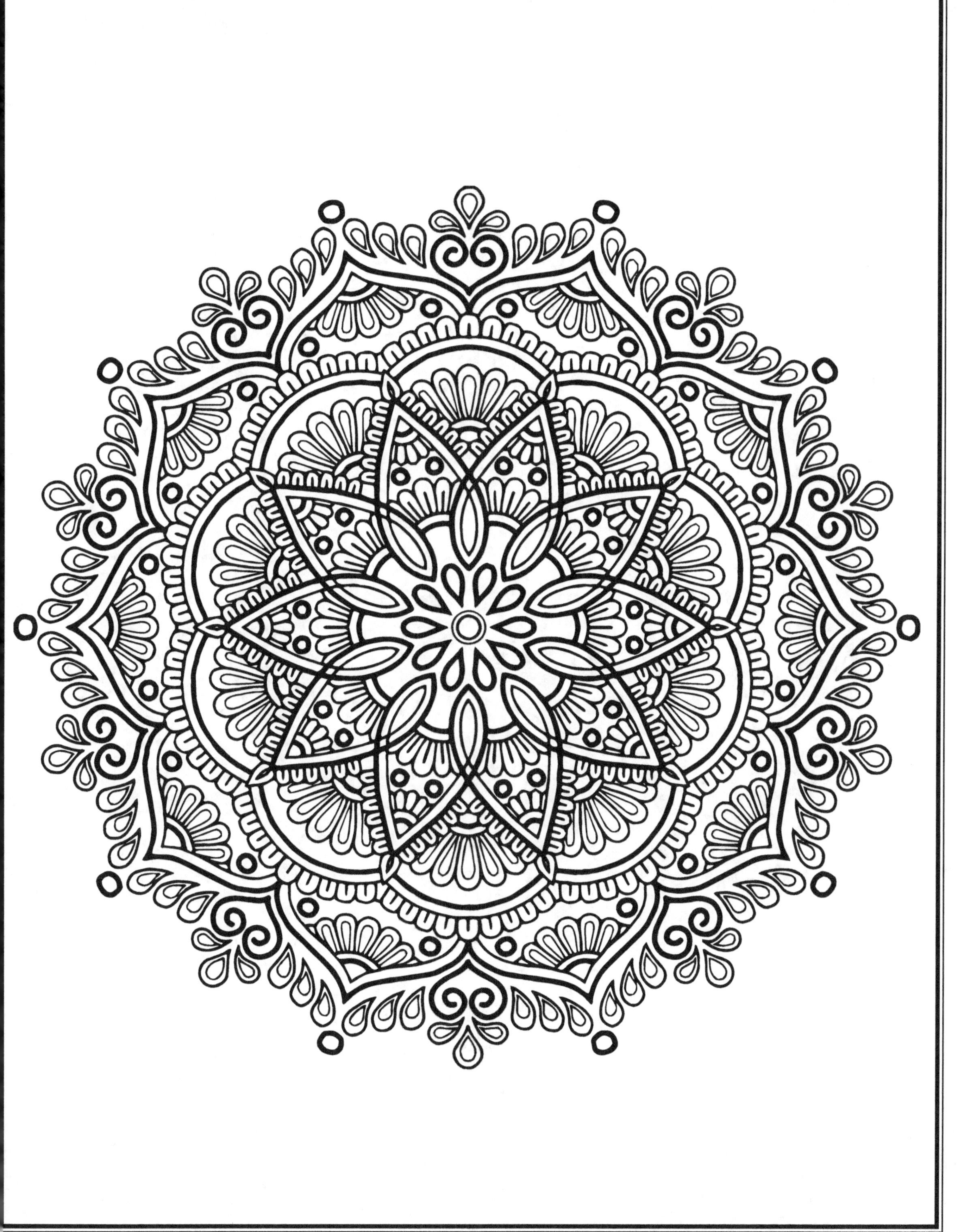

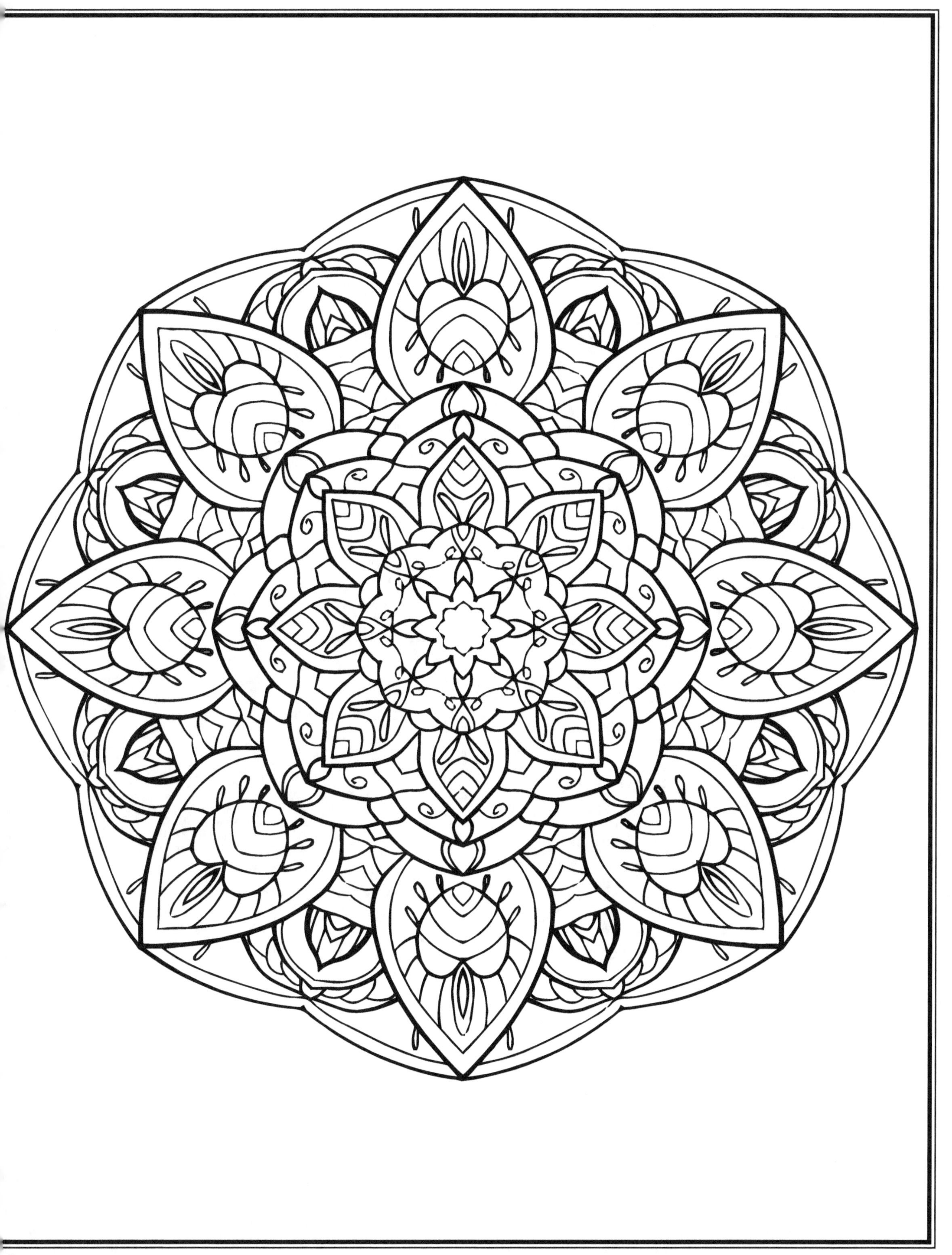

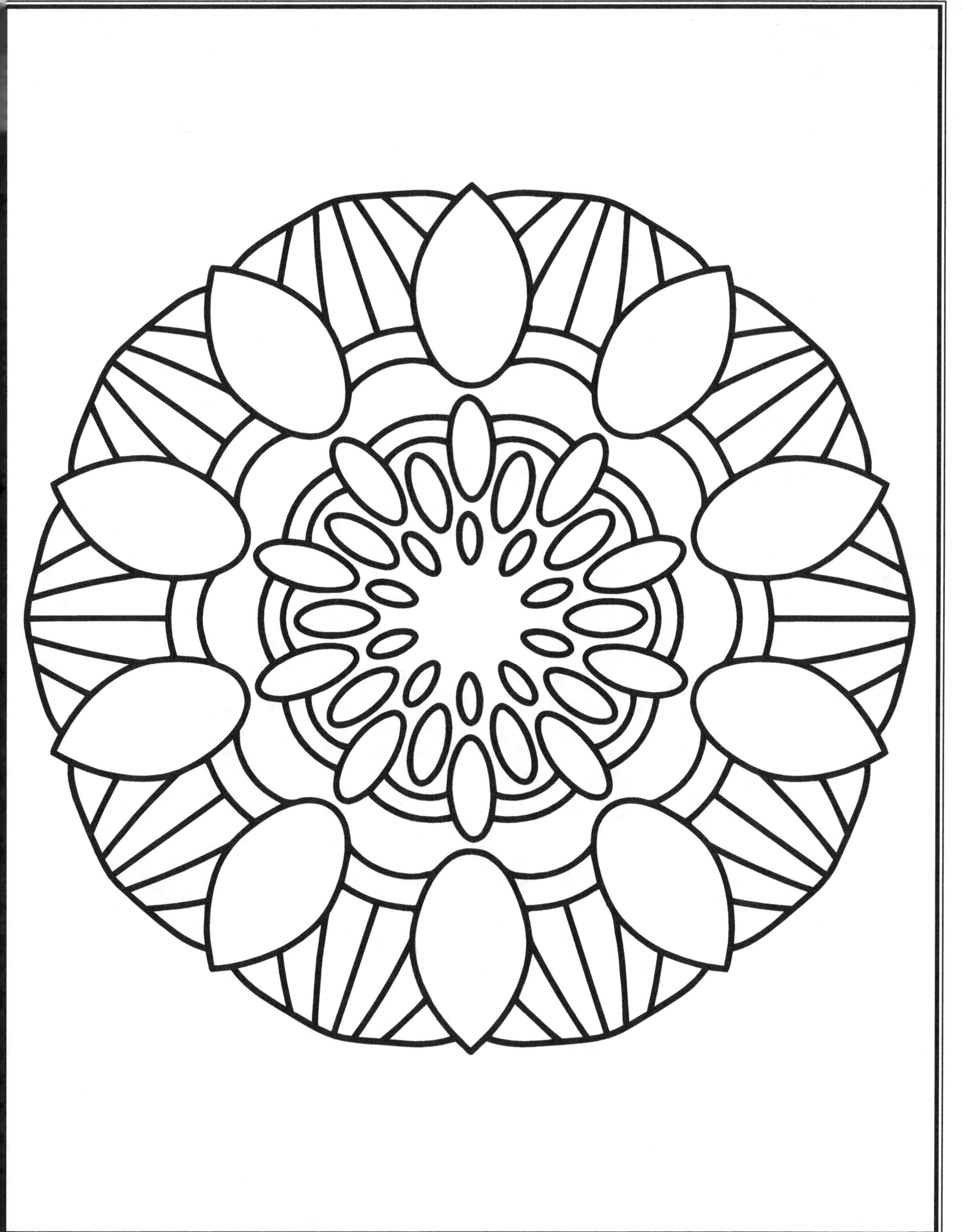

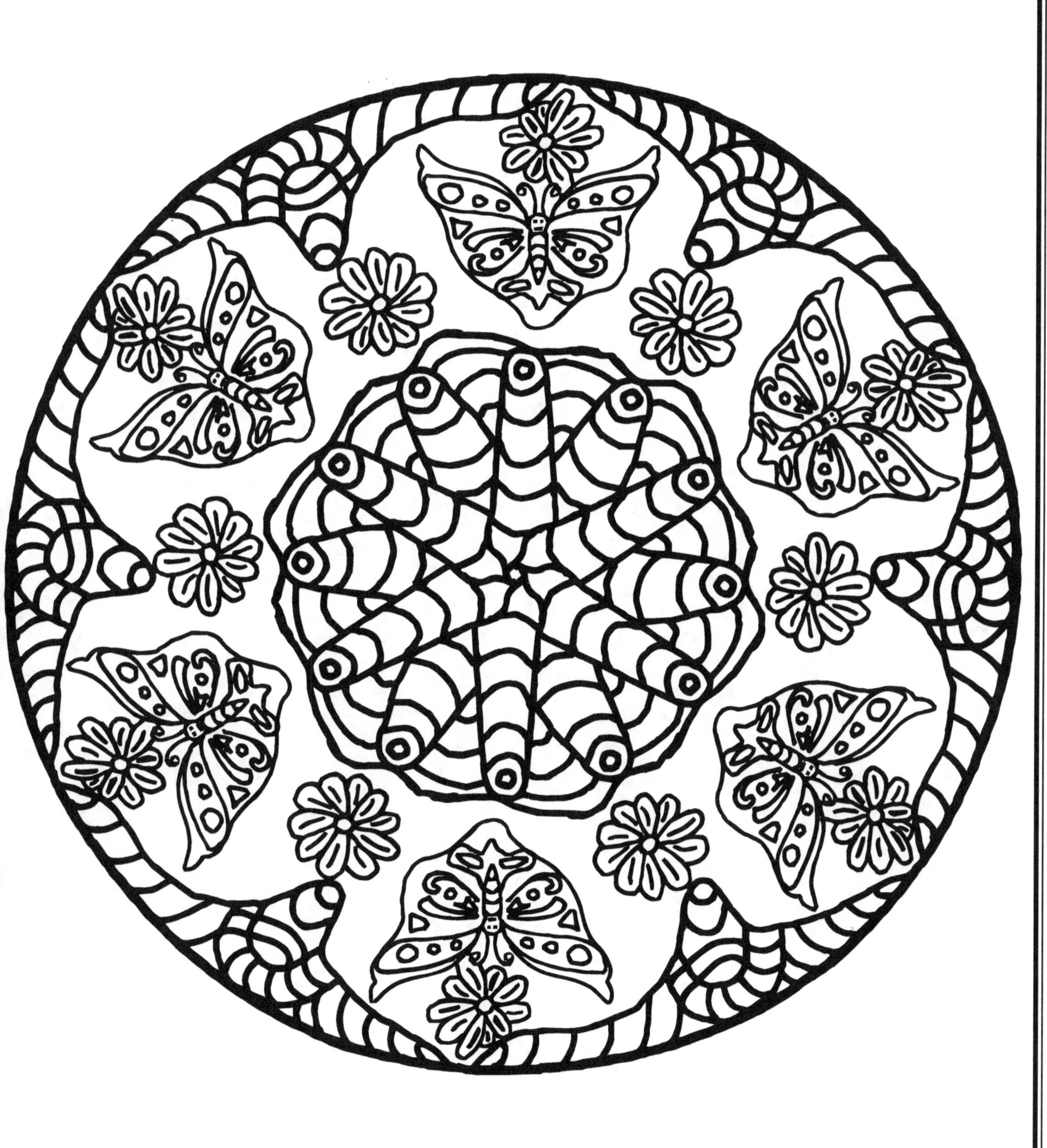

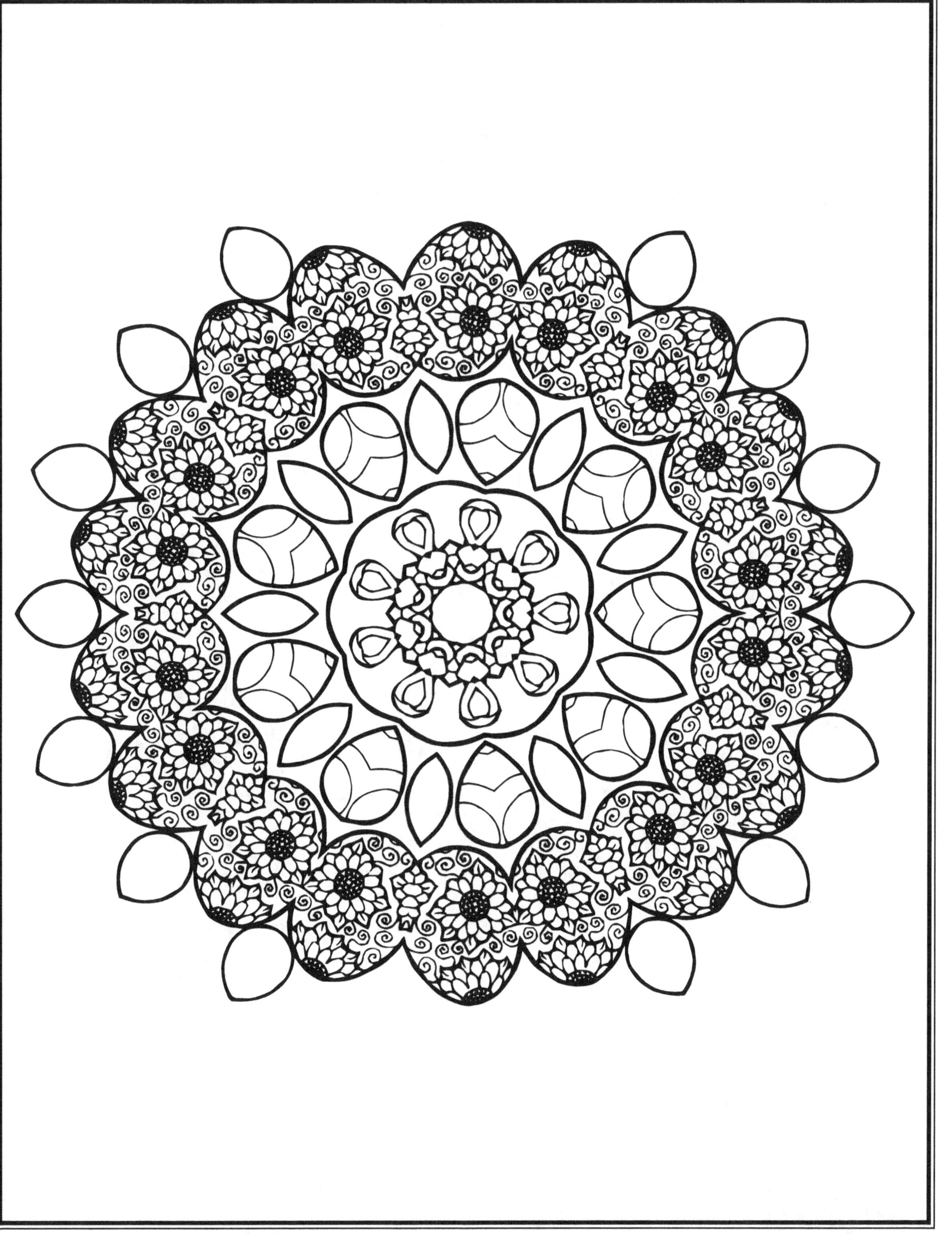

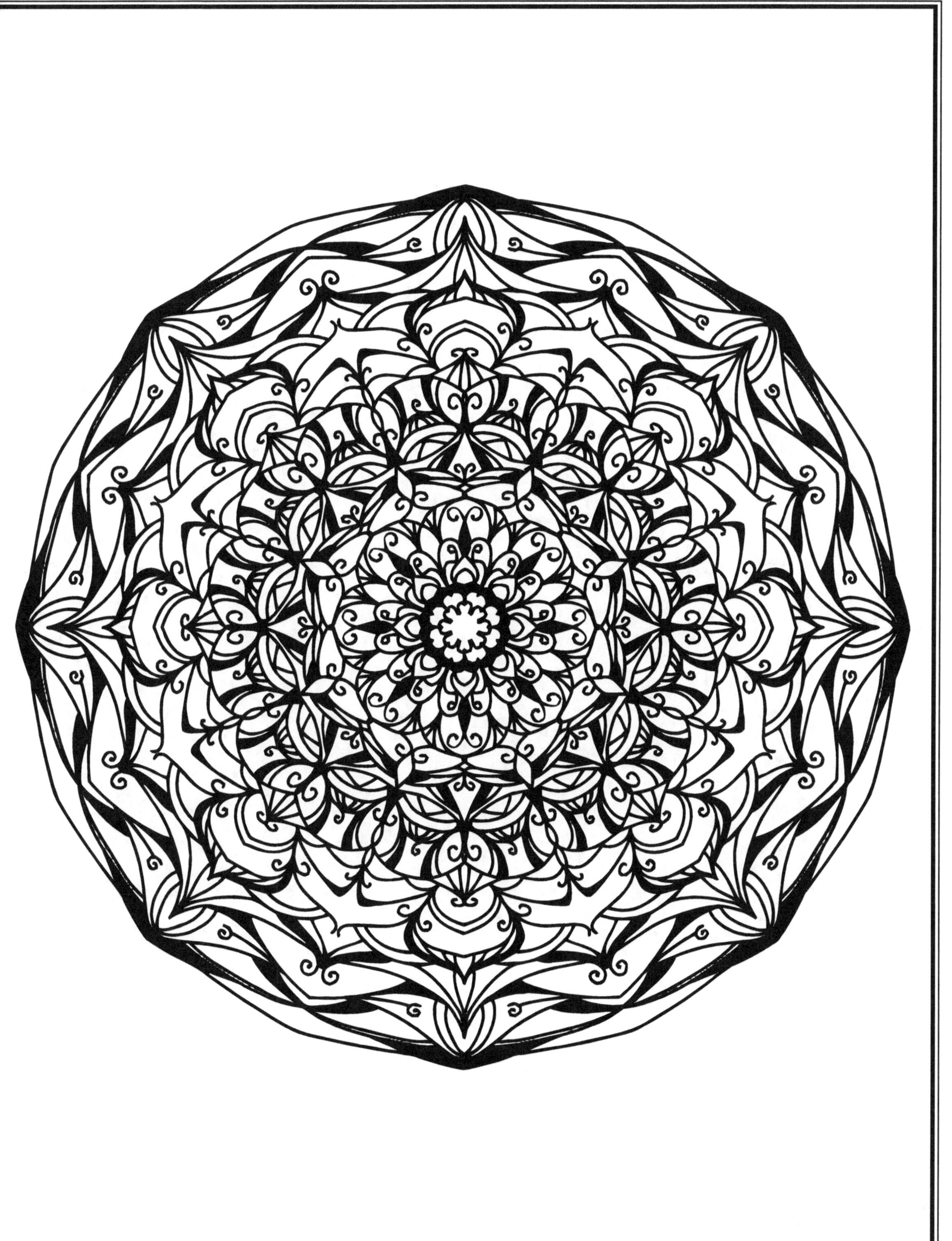

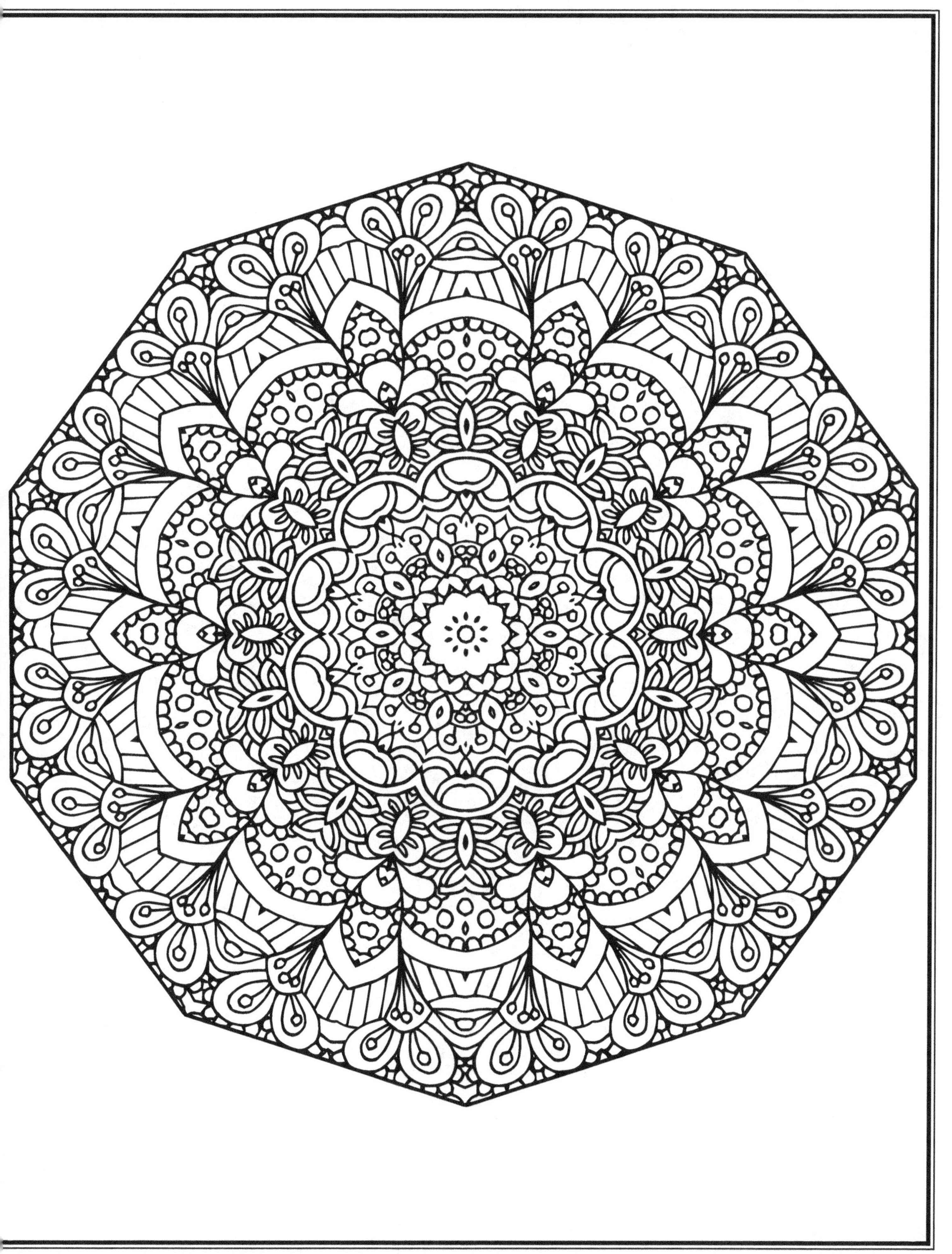

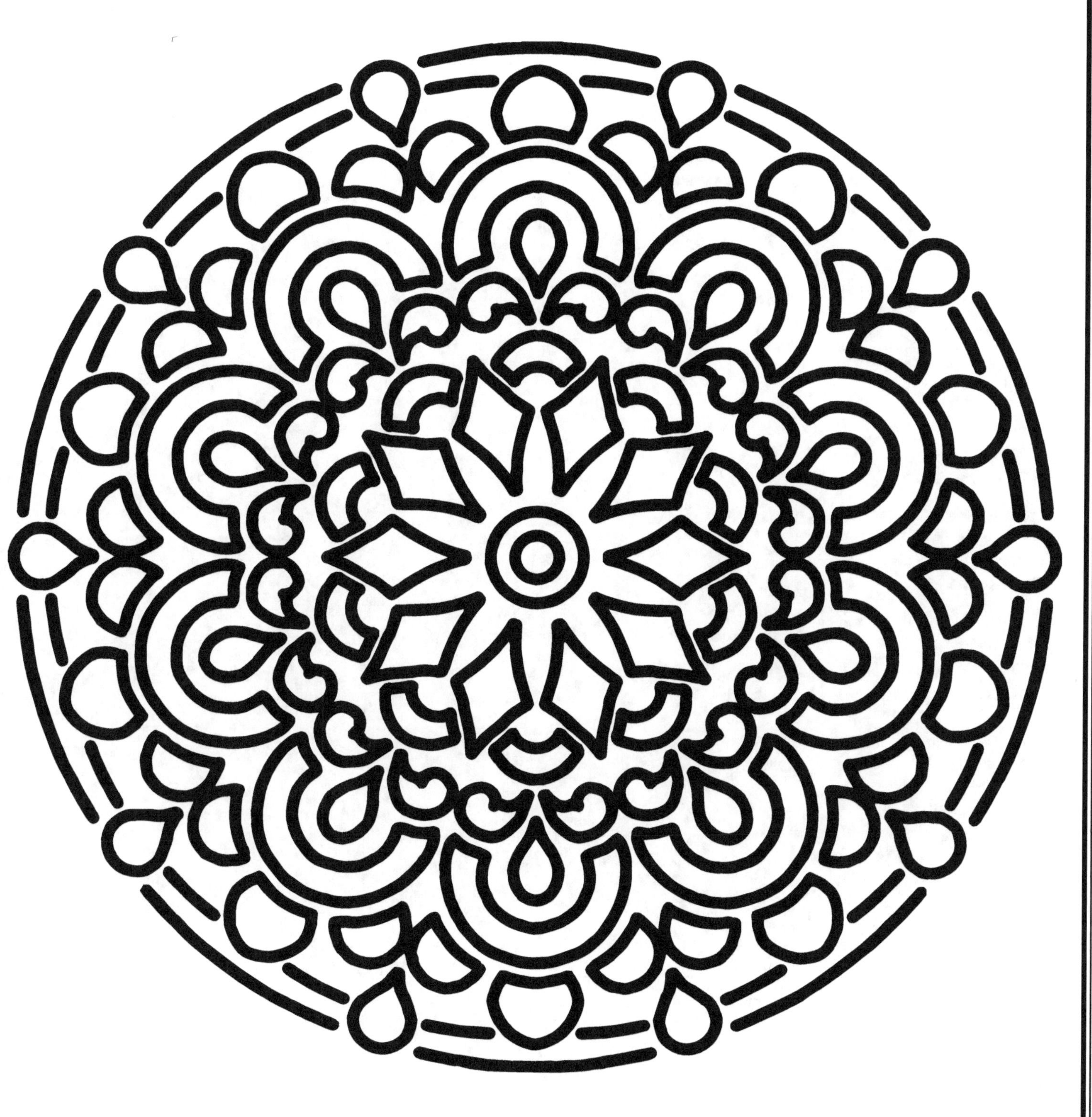

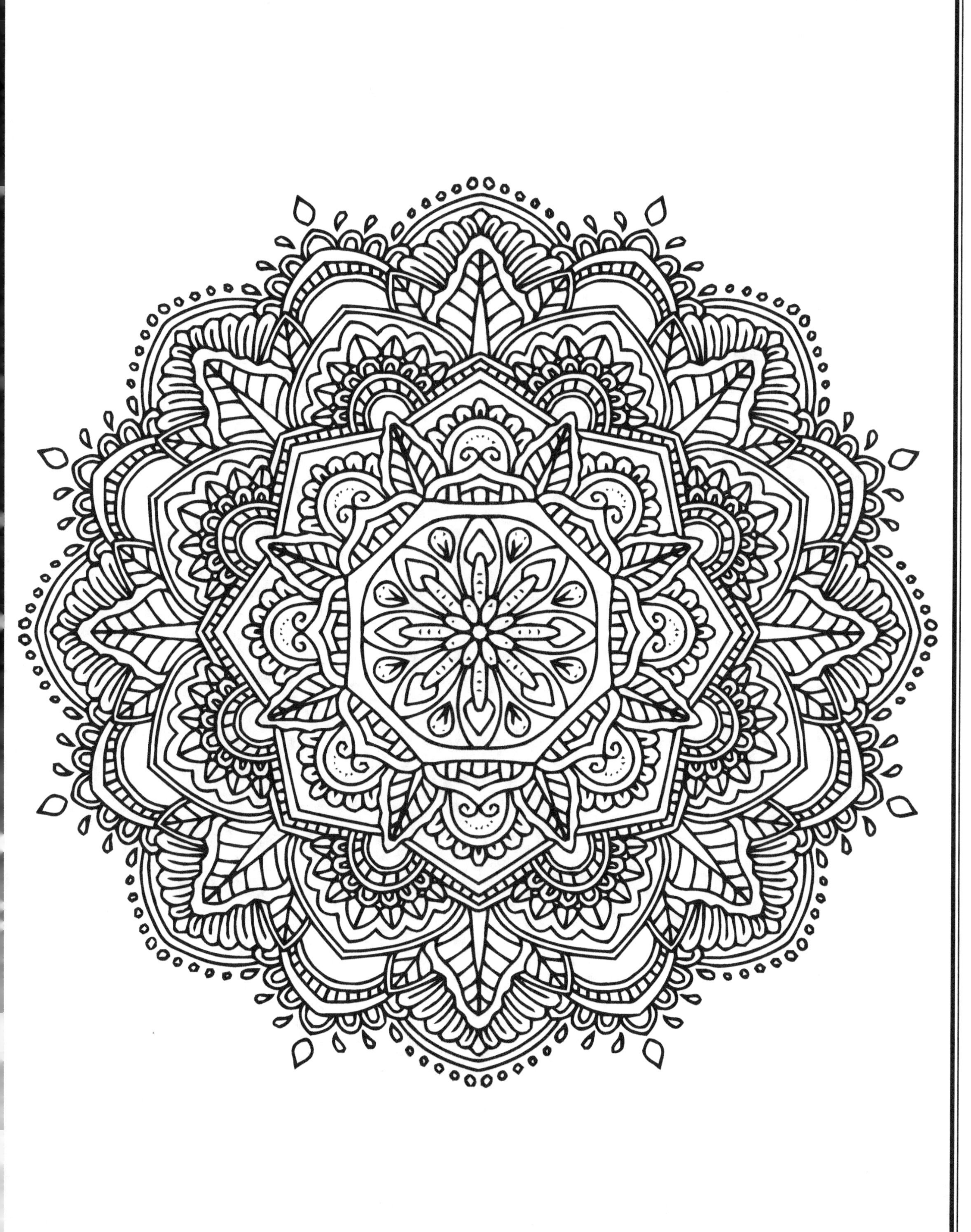

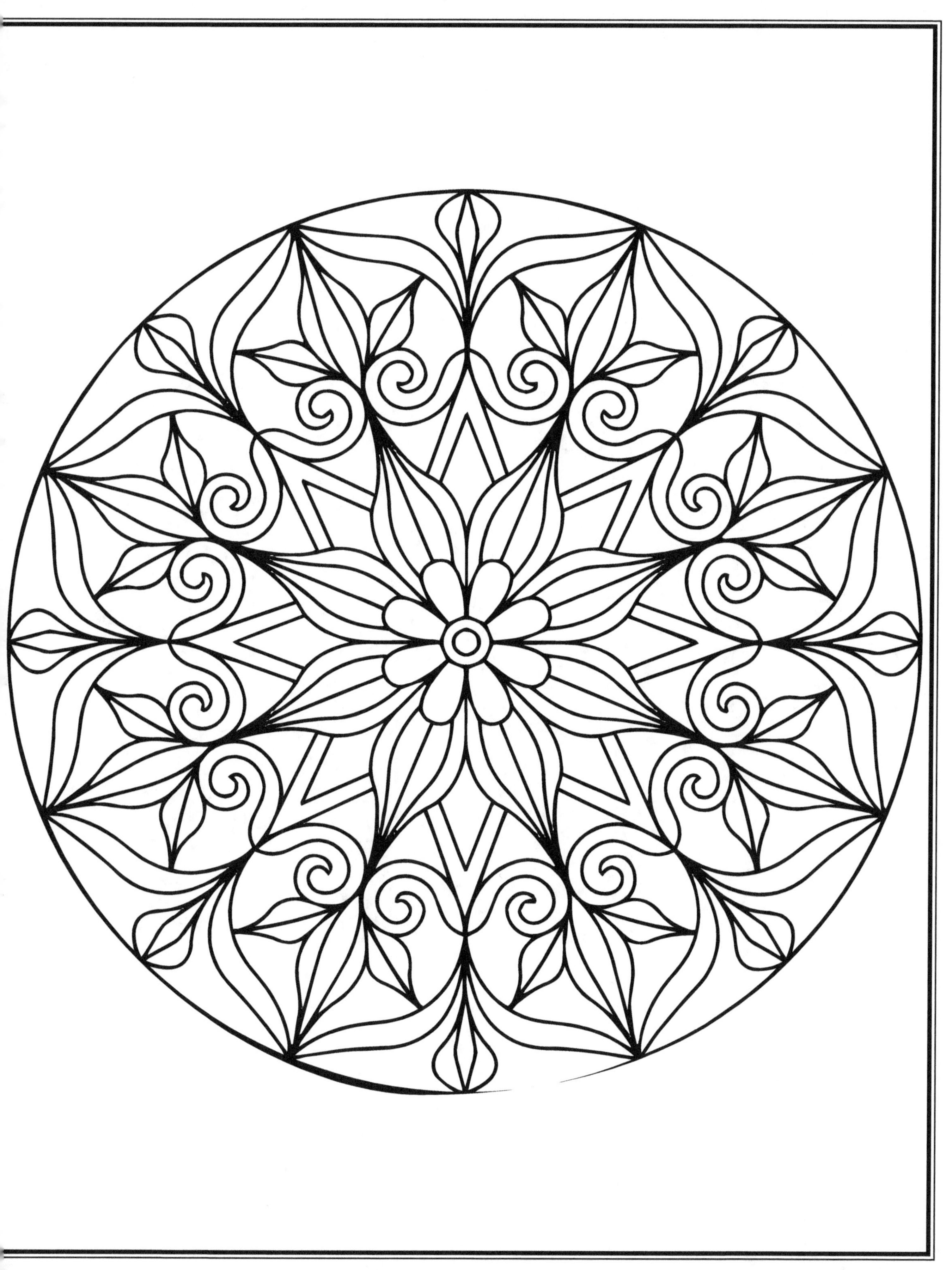

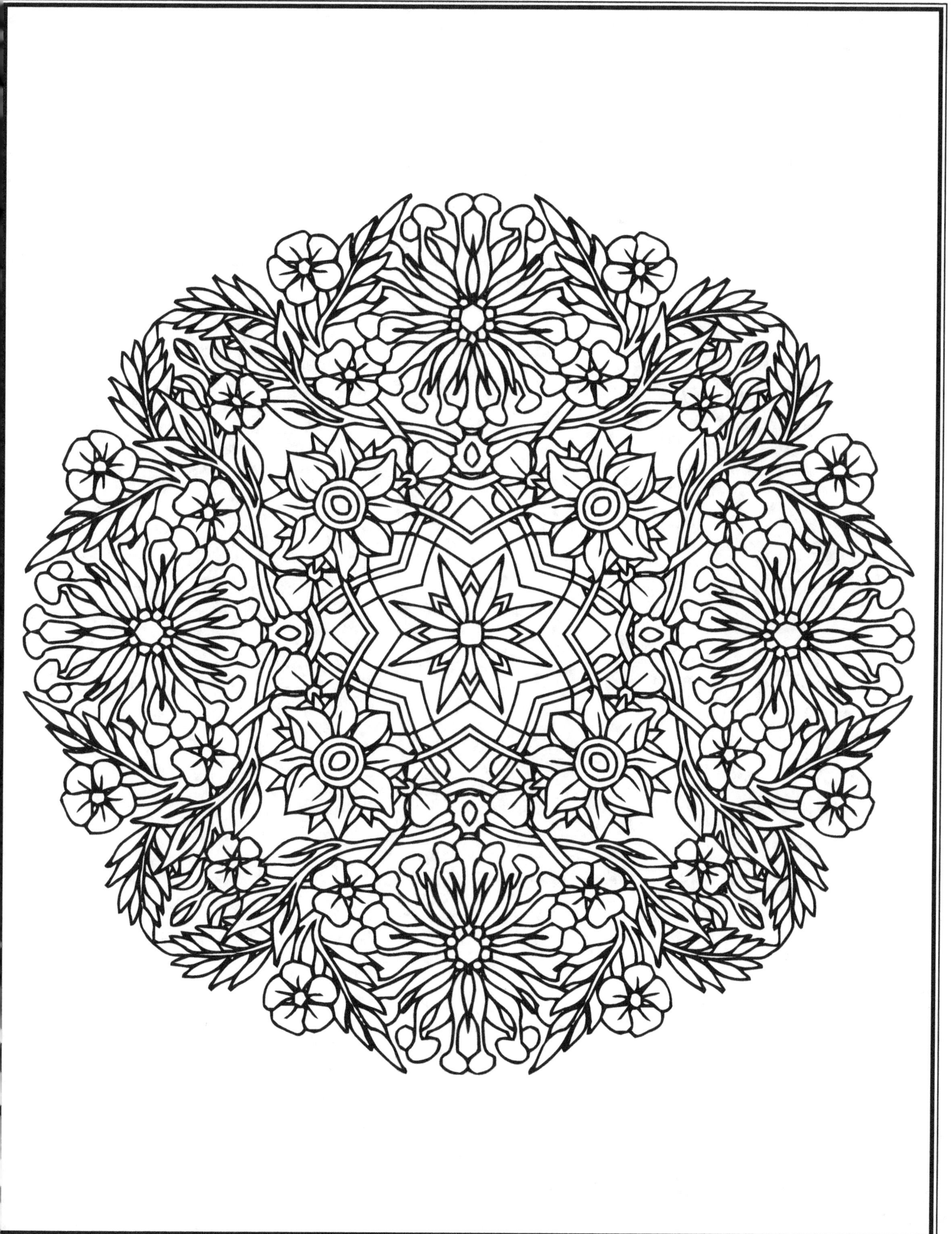

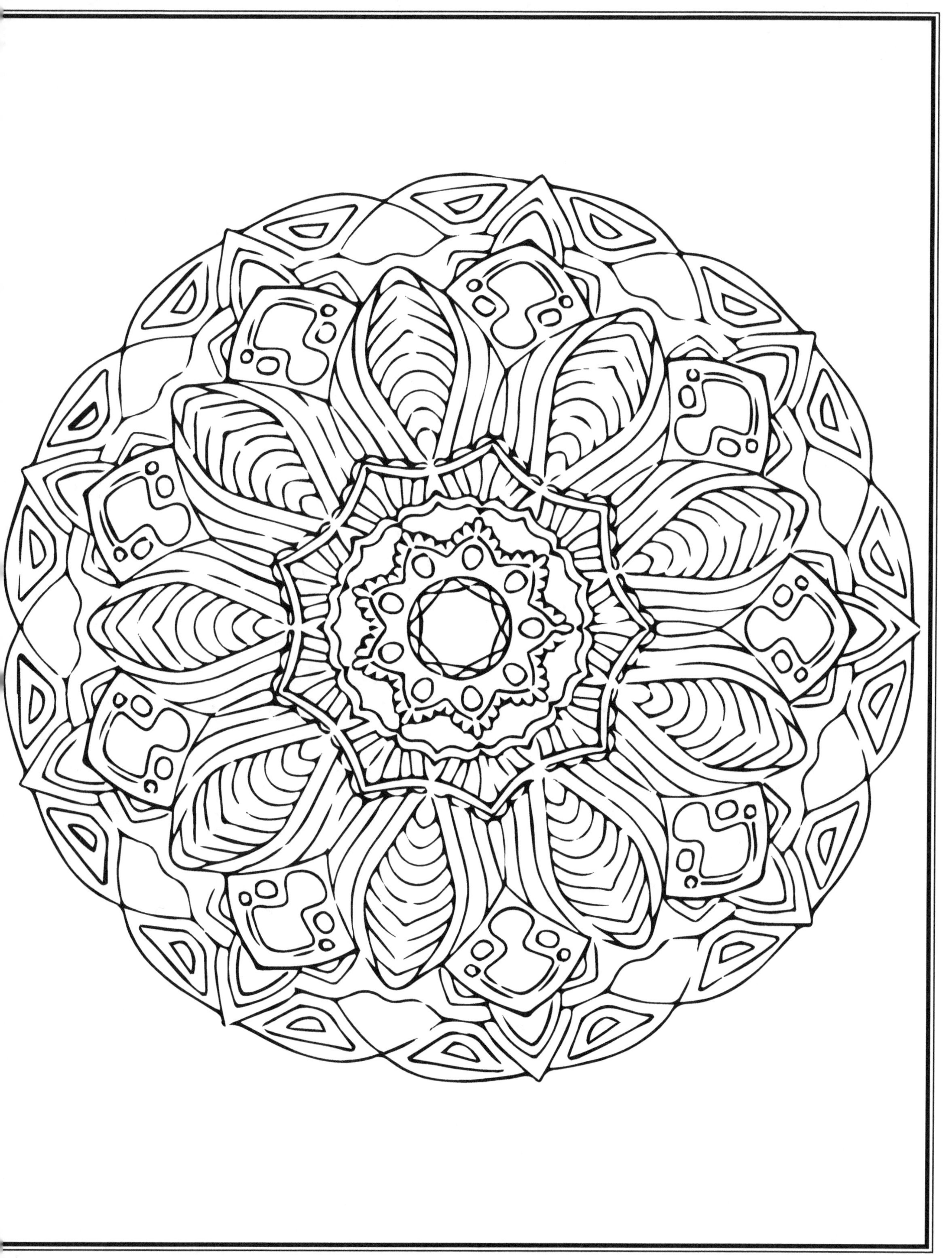

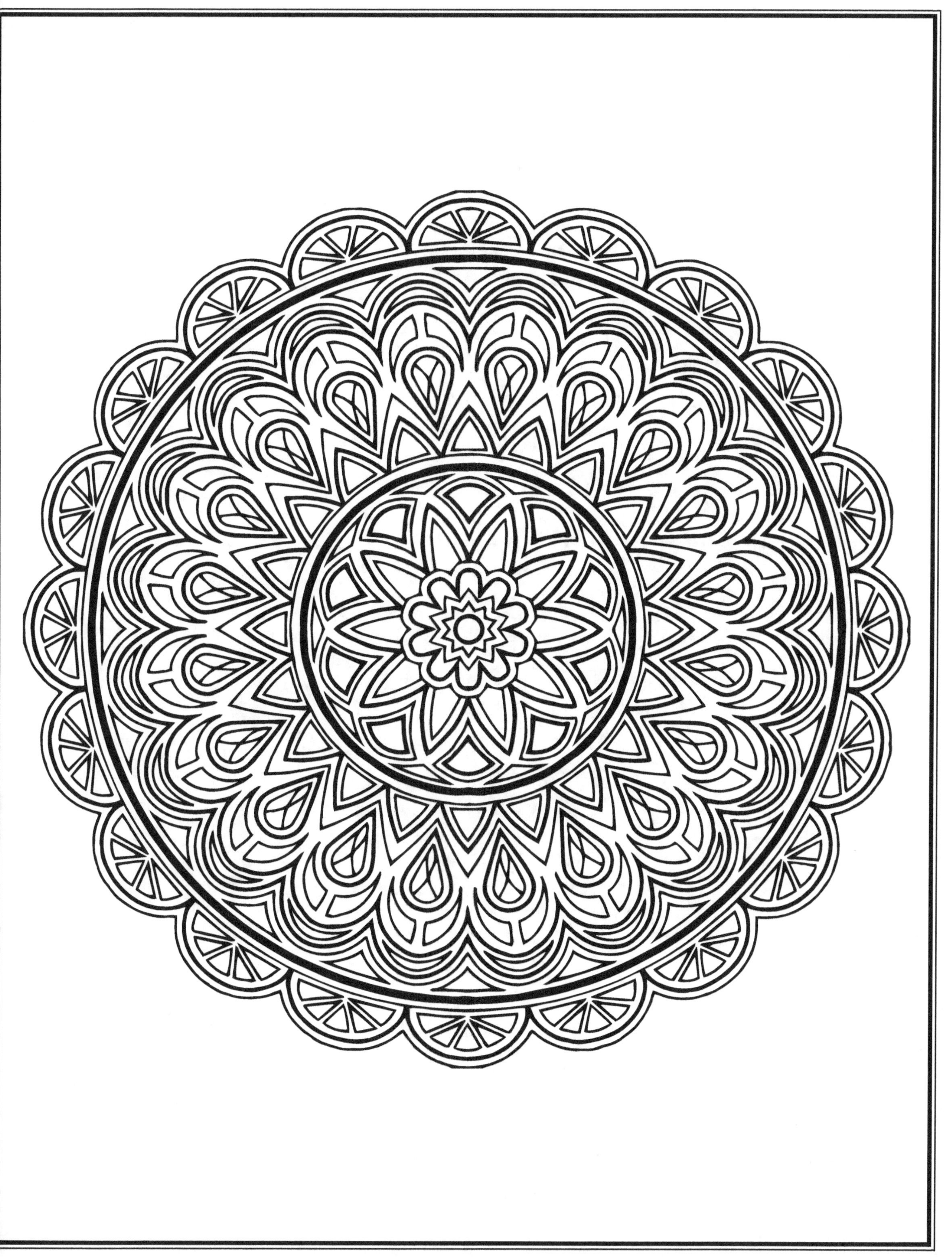

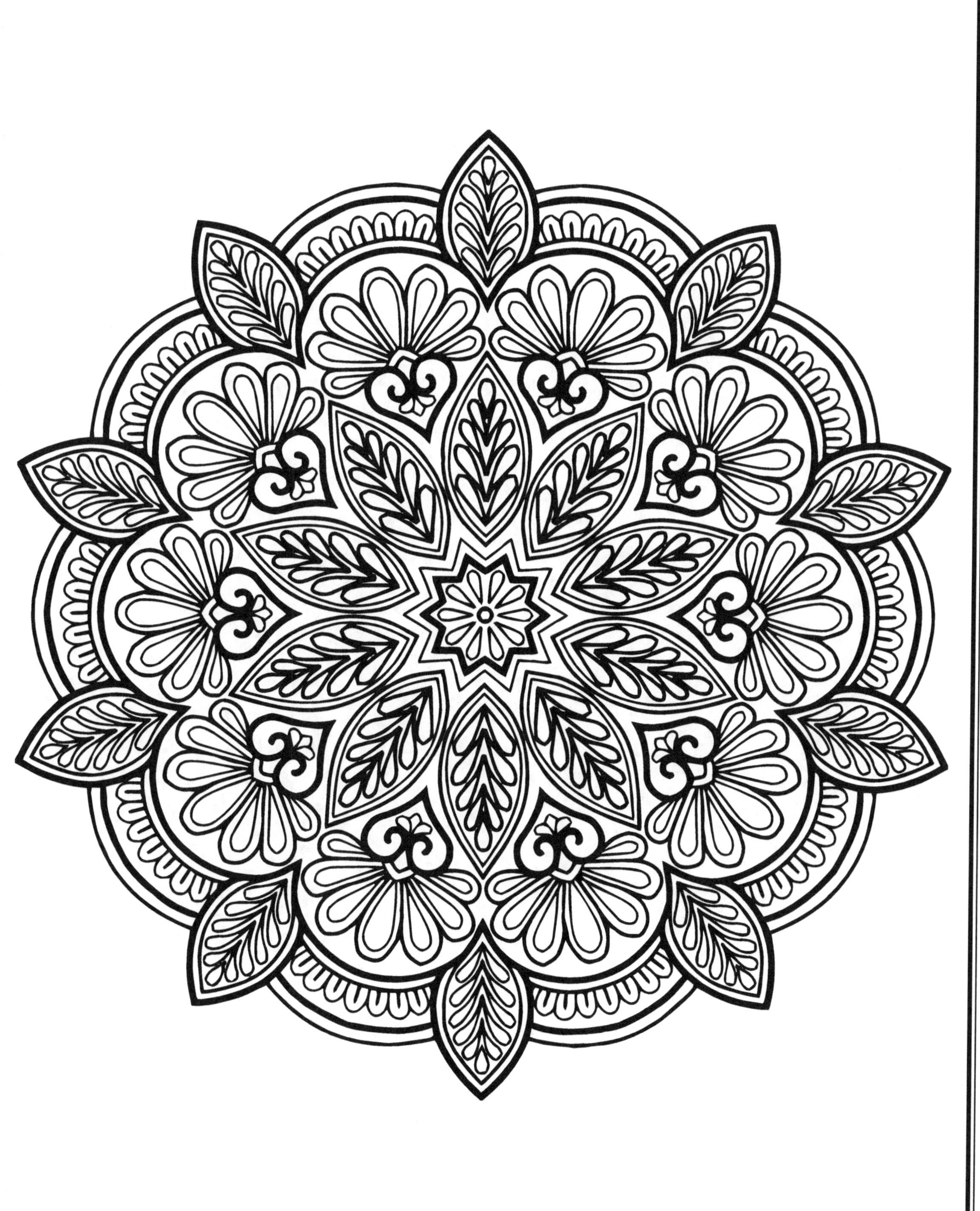

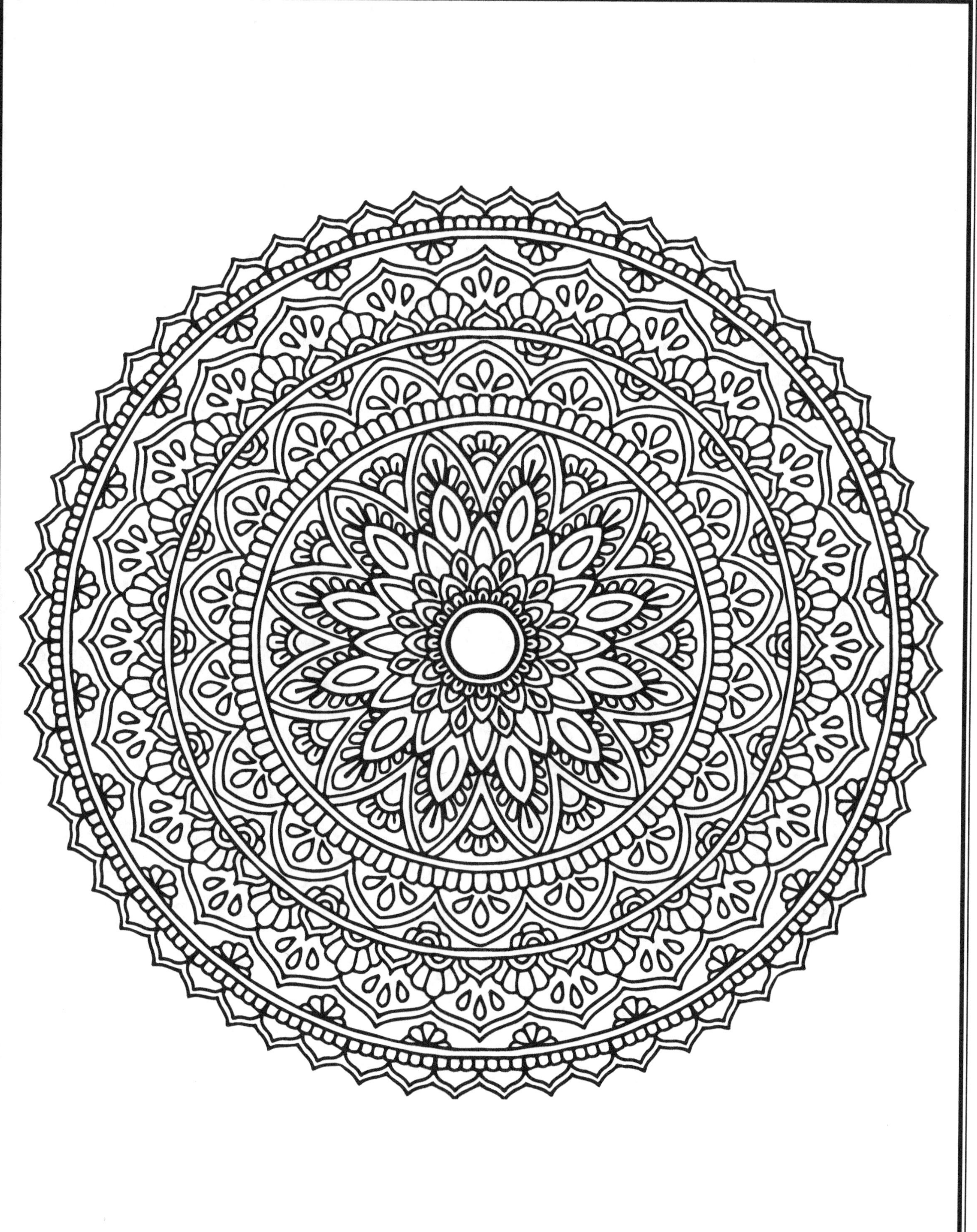

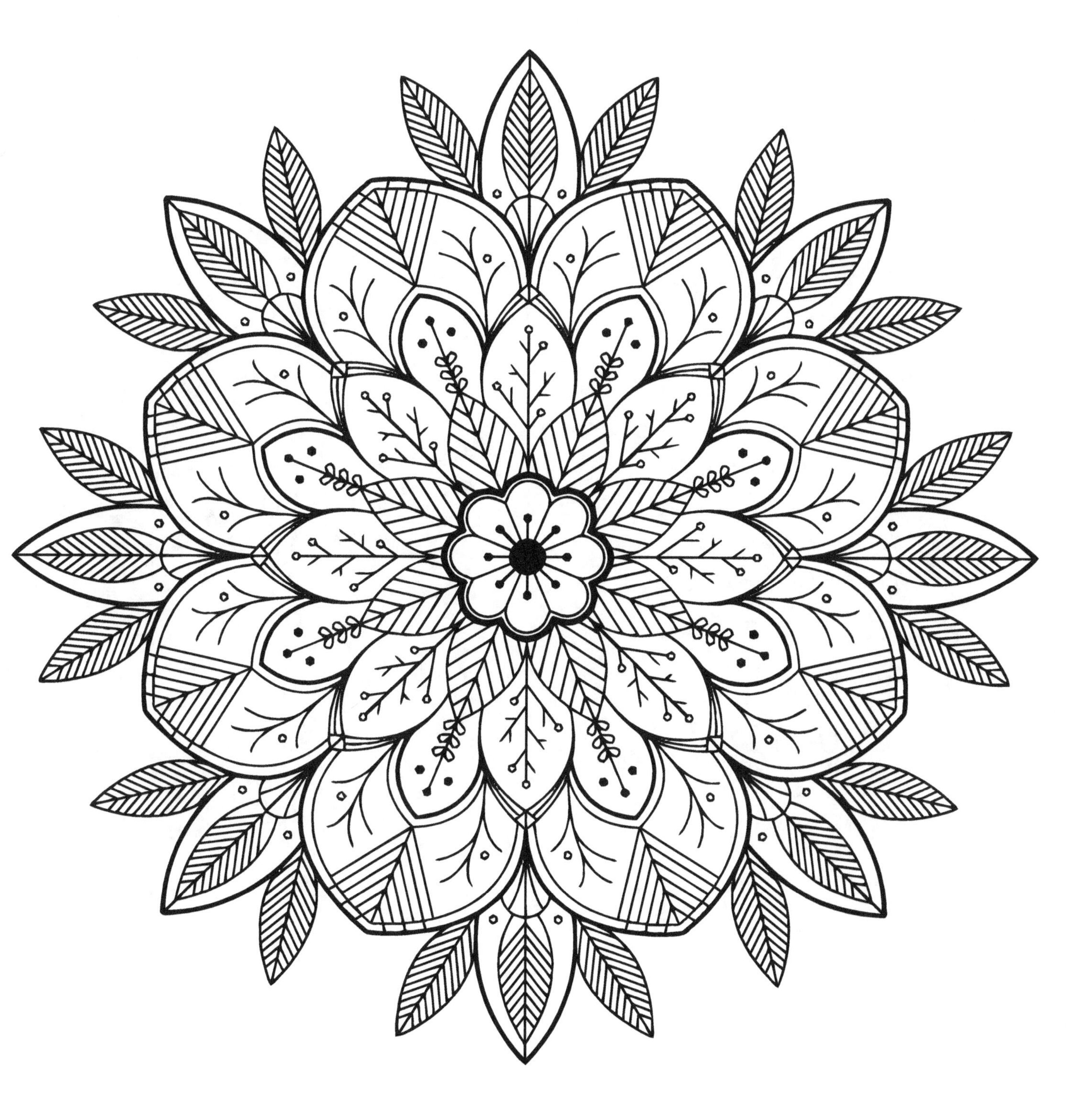

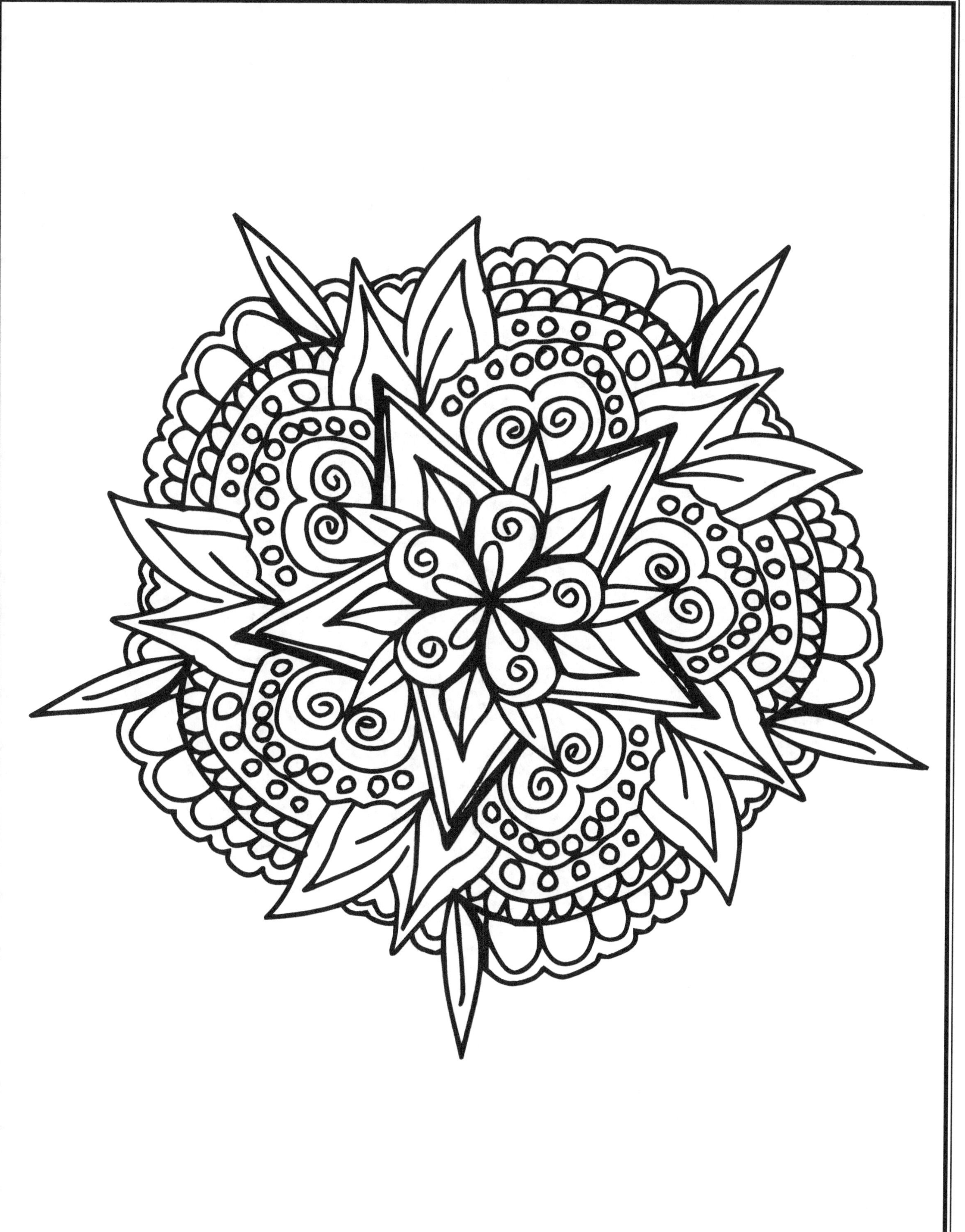

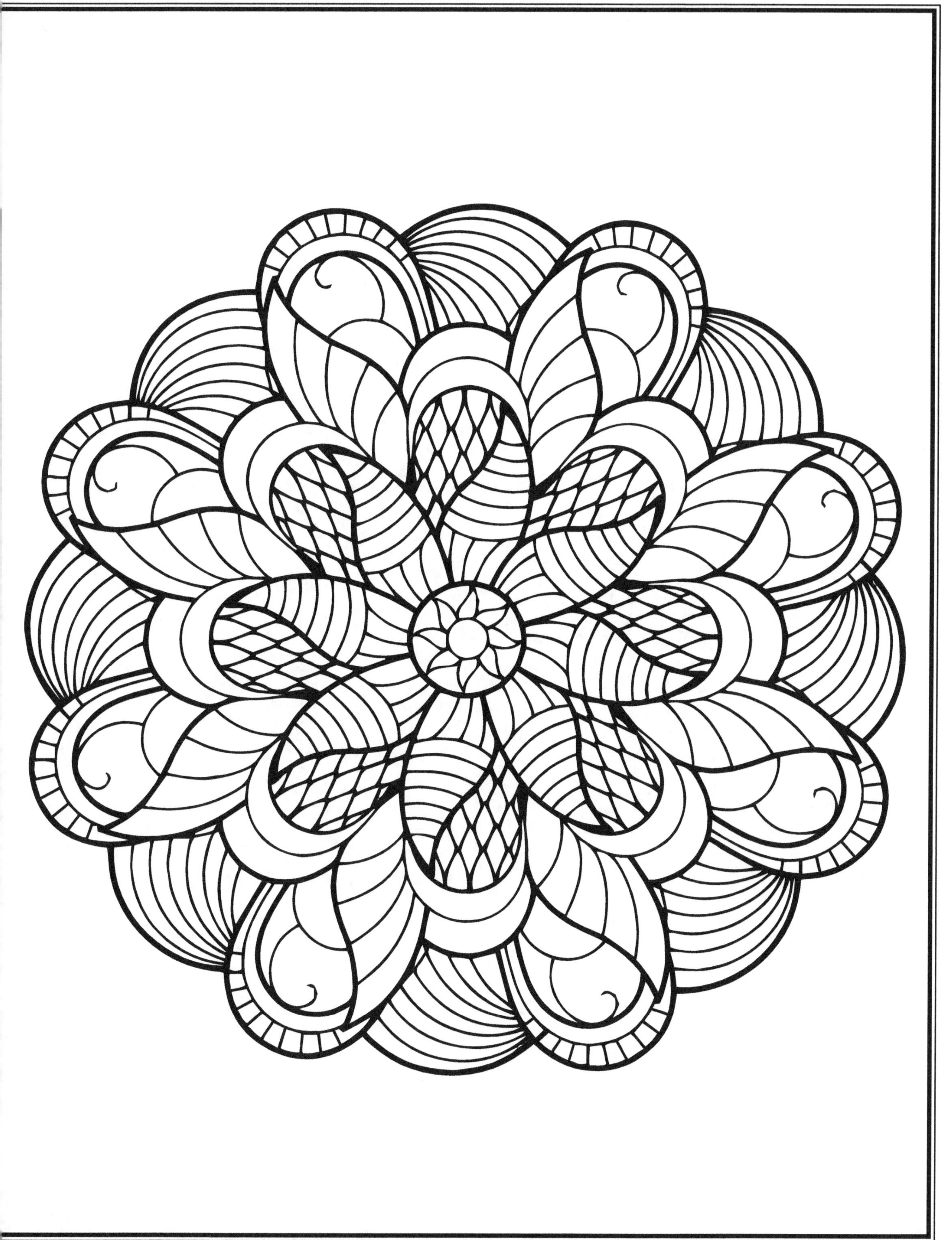

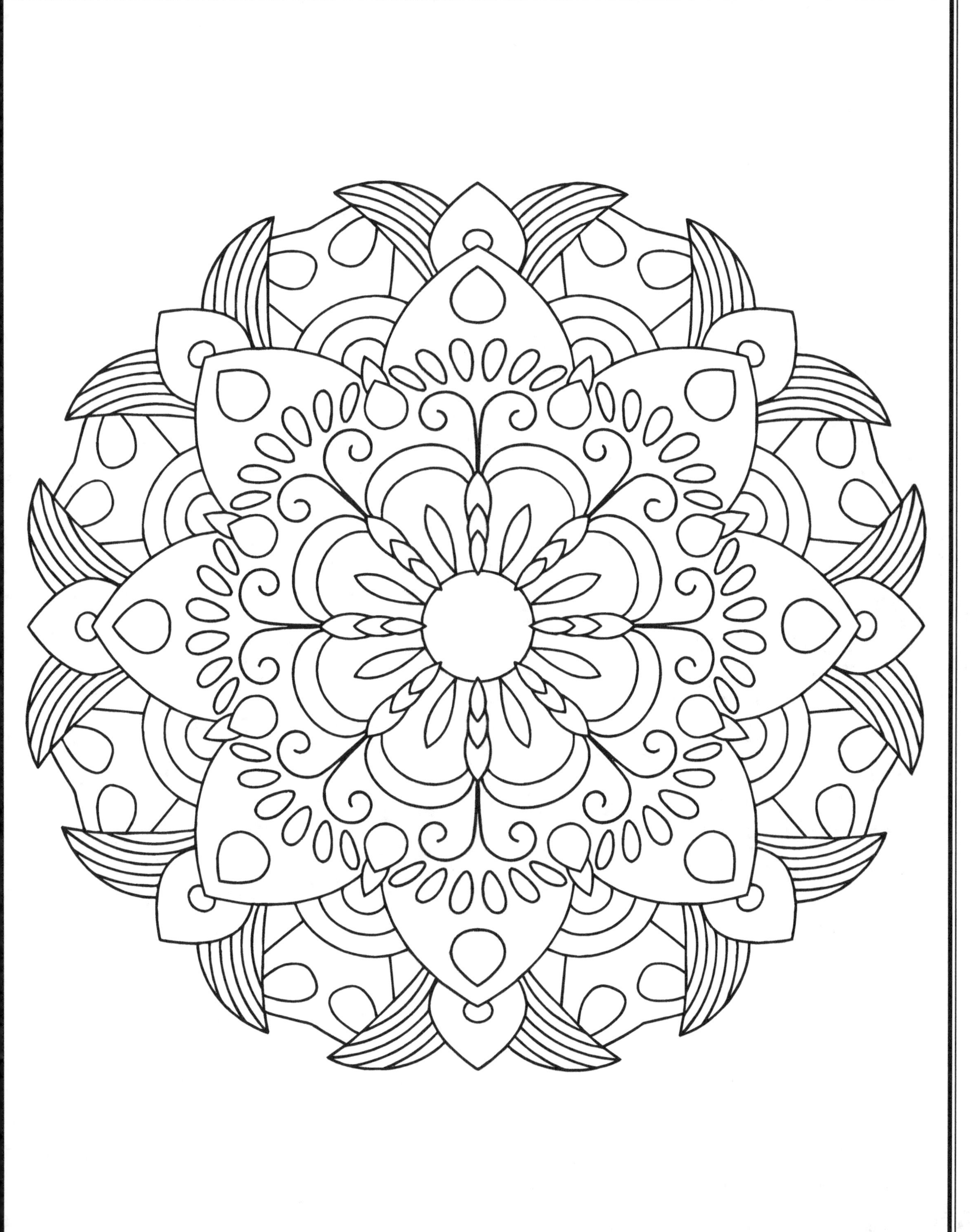